CW00732626

100 WA
Nottinghamshire

compiled by

MALCOLM SALES

The Crowood Press

First published in 1997 by
The Crowood Press Ltd
Ramsbury
Marlborough
Wiltshire SN8 2HR

British Library Cataloguing-in-Publication Data
A catalogue record for this book is
available from the British Library

ISBN 1 86126 025 3

All maps by Janet Powell

Typeset by Carreg Limited, Ross-on-Wye, Herefordshire

Printed by J W Arrowsmith Limited, Bristol

CONTENTS

PUBLISHER'S NOTE

We very much hope that you enjoy the routes presented in this book, which has been compiled with the aim of allowing you to explore the area in the best possible way - on foot.

We strongly recommend that you take the relevant map for the area, and for this reason we list the appropriate Ordnance Survey maps for each route. Whilst the details and descriptions given for each walk were accurate at time of writing, the countryside is constantly changing, and a map will be essential if, for any reason, you are unable to follow the given route. It is good practice to carry a map and use it so that you are always aware of your exact location.

We cannot be held responsible if some of the details in the route descriptions are found to be inaccurate, but should be grateful if walkers would advise us of any major alterations. Please note that whenever you are walking in the countryside you are on somebody else's land, and we must stress that you should *always* keep to established rights of way, and *never* cross fences, hedges or other boundaries unless there is a clear crossing point.

Remember the country code:

Enjoy the country and respect its life and work
Guard against all risk of fire
Fasten all gates
Keep dogs under close control
Keep to public footpaths across all farmland
Use gates and stiles to cross field boundaries
Leave all livestock, machinery and crops alone
Take your litter home
Help to keep all water clean
Protect wildlife, plants and trees
Make no unnecessary noise

The walks are listed by length - from approximately 1 to 12 miles - but the amount of time taken will depend on the fitness of the walkers and the time spent exploring any points of interest along the way. Nearly all the walks are circular and most offer recommendations for refreshments.

Good walking.

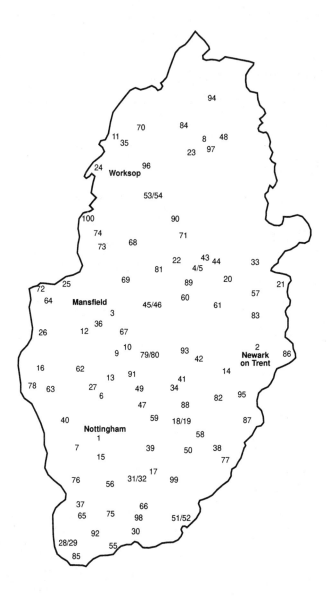

Walk 1   NOTTINGHAM $1\frac{1}{2}$m (2km)

Maps: OS Sheets Landranger 129; Pathfinder 833.
A walk through historic Nottingham.
Start: At 569396, Nottingham Castle.

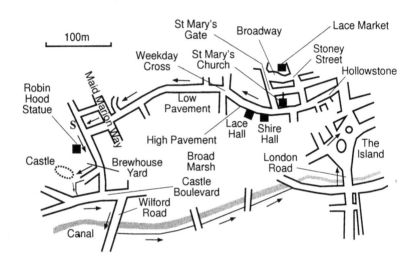

From the entrance to **Nottingham Castle**, where the Robin Hood Way also starts, turn right and walk south-eastwards along Castle Road to the statue of Robin Hood. Looking back at the Castle the walker will see the outer bailey bridge spanning the now dry moat. Opposite the statue is the Lace Centre. Continue along Castle Road to **The Trip To Jerusalem**. Turn right into **Brewhouse Yard**. Cross the yard looking behind to **Castle Rock**. On reaching Castle Boulevard, cross and turn left. Turn right along Wilford Road, crossing the Nottingham Canal. From the bridge there is a good view of Castle Lock. Turn right on to the canal towpath and right again to walk eastwards along the canal's southern bank. The catches of the anglers prove the healthy condition of the water. Follow the towpath past the new Magistrates Courts and the old British Waterways building. Beyond, the towpath becomes a quiet preserve of walkers and anglers: you will get a glimpse of the Council House and the Lace Market.

The canal bends sharply right: climb steps to London Road and go northwards to reach The Island. From the road you will see **St Mary's Church** towering above the surrounding buildings. Cross The Island and continue along London Road. Turn left into Hollowstone and continue to St Mary's Church. Turn right into Stoney Street and walk to Broadway. Walking through Broadway in the heart of the old lace area is to experience the grandeur this industry brought to Nottingham. Turn left into St Mary's Gate to return to St Mary's Church.

Turn right along High Pavement, passing **Shire Hall**, now a museum, to reach **The Lace Hall**. Continue along High Pavement to **Weekday Cross**. Now cross Middle Hill into Low Pavement and walk westwards to Castle Gate. Along this road you will pass notice boards giving the brief history of the area. At the junction of Castle Gate and Maid Marian Way you will reach the Royal Children Inn. Opposite is St Nicholas' Church. During the Civil War, Hutchinson had the church tower demolished to prevent Royalist soldiers shooting into the Castle. Cross Maid Marian Way at a pedestrian crossing and continue along Castle Gate to return to the Castle.

POINTS OF INTEREST:

Nottingham Castle – The first castle on this site was built in 1068 by William Peverel on the orders of William the Conqueror. Under Henry II it became the chief royal fortress in the Midlands. During the Civil War, Colonel John Hutchinson maintained a Parliamentarian stronghold here.

The Trip To Jerusalem – This is one of the oldest inns in Nottingham. It was a calling place for the Crusaders on their way to the Holy Land. It has rooms and cellars and a chimney cut into the rock on which the castle is built.

Brewhouse Yard – Many local plants are grown in the gardens around the yard.

Castle Rock – The caves in the rock were once the home of the ancient Britons

St Mary's Church – Samuel Booth married Sarah here in 1797. Their son William started the Salvation Army movement.

Shire Hall – Now a museum called called 'The Galleries of Justice'. Public hangings were carried out here until 1864.

The Lace Hall – This former church has a cafe inside overlooking a museum to lace making.

Weekday Cross – This is the site of the former weekday market. The Town Hall, jail and stocks were once situated here.

REFRESHMENTS:

There is something for everyone in Nottingham.

Walk 2   NEWARK   2m (3km)

Maps: OS Sheets Landranger 121; Pathfinder 796 and 797.
A short walk through historic Newark.
Start: At 792533, the Sconce Hills car park.

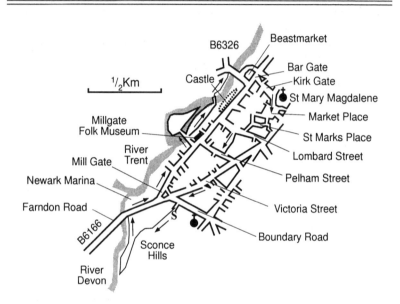

Walk south-westwards along the tarmac path through the children's playing area into the open ground of **Sconce Hills**. Continue through the recreational area to reach the bank of the River Devon. Now turn back and walk along the bank of this tranquil river, heading towards the B6166 and passing fishermen enjoying their sport. Cross the road, with care, and turn right along it to reach the Spring House junction, passing Newark Marina.

Go left along **Millgate**, turning left to visit the **Millgate Folk Museum**. Leave the museum and go down Mill Lane. Cross the **River Trent** to reach Huddlestone Wharf. The bridge gives a good view of **Newark Castle**. Now walk along Huddlestone Wharf to reach Newark Town Lock and a British Waterways dry dock. Turn right along the B6326, recross the Trent to reach Beastmarket. On market days there is a flea market in the car park here. Walk through the market, passing the Victorian wharf buildings to reach Bar Gate. Cross Bar Gate and walk up Kirk Gate with the spire of St Mary Magdalene Church towering 77 metres (252 feet) above the street. Go past the Tudor 'Charles I Coffee House', and continue to reach the church in Church Street. Now go through to the Market Place.

Cross the Market Place to reach the exquisite building housing the Nottingham Building Society. Walk beside the building into Ye Old White Hart Yard, then turn right into St Marks Place.

Now turn left into St Marks Lane, then cross Lombard Street and walk through a car park to reach Pelham Street. Turn left and walk to Victoria Street. Now turn right and walk along Victoria Street to reach Boundary Road and the Sconce Hill car park.

POINTS OF INTEREST:

Sconce Hills – In the Civil War this was an encampment for the Royalists. It is one of the best surviving examples of military engineering from the period.

Millgate – This is a fine area of Victorian buildings with an active Conservation Society. Look out for Blyton's Yard and Porter's Yard.

Millgate Folk Museum – The museum shows examples of life in Newark when agriculture was much more of a prominent employer than it is today.

River Trent – Before the arrival of the railway, the river was a major form of transport for commerce. Wool, coal and agricultural produce passed through the town on route for Nottingham or more distant destinations.

Newark Castle – This was always an important defence position as it stands at the junction of two major routes, the Great North Road and the Fosse Way. In Norman times the Bishop of Lincoln rebuilt the castle. King John came here to die. It became a ruin after the various battles and sieges of the Civil War when Newark stayed loyal to King Charles.

REFRESHMENTS:

The Spring House, Millgate.
The Water Mill, Millgate.
Ye Old White Hart Yard, White Hart Yard.
Charles I Coffee House, Kirk Gate.

Walk 3 **STRAWBERRY HILL** 2¹/₂m (4km)

Maps: OS Sheets Landranger 120; Pathfinder 779 and 795.
A quite and colourful Autumn woodland walk.
Start: At 583594, in Helmsley Road, Rainworth.

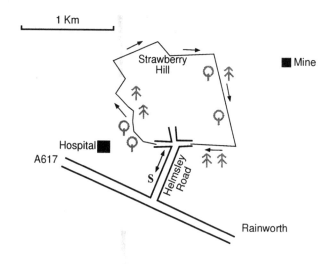

Car parking is possible in Helmesley Road: please park considerately. The walk starts from the end of the road. Walk northwards along the unmade road, passing stables on the right, to reach a metal barrier. Turn left along a bridleway, following the edge of the woodland. After 200 yards the path splits: turn right (northwards) and follow a broad path into the woods. At a crossing of paths, bear left (north-westwards) to continue along the major path. On this path there are conifer trees to the right and deciduous trees to the left.

Follow the path to a T-junction. Turn right, and, after 50 yards you will reach a metal fence on the left guarding some open cast mine workings. At this point the path veers north-eastwards and broadens significantly. Leave the metal fence when it turns sharp left, keeping to the major track and following a line of telegraph poles. At the next path crossing, turn left, uphill. The top of Strawberry Hill is about 100 yards ahead and you have a choice of routes. Either go direct to the top along a narrow path or follow a broader track that circles the top. Strawberry Hill is covered in deciduous trees, so you will be denied any significant views, particularly in summer.

Go over the top of the hill to join the circular path on the northern side. Turn right, eastwards, to go along a broad path. Go straight over at a path crossing, continuing for a further 100 yards to reach a T-junction. Ahead here is a dilapidated fence guarding British Coal property: turn right (southwards), keeping the fence on your left, even when it performs a zig-zag. Now, at the point where the fence goes sharp left, descend a steep hill for 50 yards to reach a T-junction with a broad track. Turn left for 25 yards and then turn right along a path going through the coniferous woods.

Follow the path to reach a T-junction at the edge of the woods. Turn right (westwards) and go along a wide bridleway that forms the boundary between the woods and some paddocks. This path will bring you back to the metal barrier near the start of the walk: reverse the outward journey back to Helmsley Road.

POINTS OF INTEREST:
This walk offers a fine view of a typical East Midland open cast mine at work, and even finer views of the woodlands's rich colours in Autumn. The woodland fungi will also keep the keen naturalist occupied.

REFRESHMENTS:
Nothing on the walk, but Rainworth has plenty of opportunities.

MILL FIELD $2\frac{1}{2}$m (4km)
or 6m (10km)

Maps: OS Sheets Landranger 120; Pathfinder 780.
A walk of historical interest with good views.
Start: At 724670, the Laxton Information Centre car park.

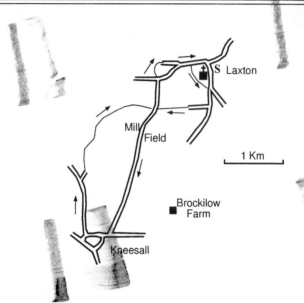

Leave the car park, beside the Dovecote Inn and the Information Centre, and cross the village green, walking towards the 12th-century Church of St Michael. Turn left and follow the footpath through the churchyard and into the field beyond. The yellow footpath signs now lead you across several grassy fields to reach a road opposite Manor Farm. Turn right along the road for 150 yards, then turn right again to go along a green lane. The lane becomes a path: follow it through a wooded area to reach a field. Maintain direction to reach a plaque in Mill Field giving information about the farming practices of this area.

The shorter walk goes right towards **Laxton**. The longer walk goes left, but returns to this point. To return to Laxton, follow the route description in the final paragraph.

The longer walk turns left, following a green lane as it dips down to cross a ditch and then goes over a ridge. Beyond the ridge the lane drops down again to reach a road (the Ossington road) on the outskirts of Kneesall. As you emerge on to the road you will find a seat waiting to welcome you. Turn right and walk along the road into Kneesall. By the corner of School Lane you will see an old water pump in the orchard. In the village, turn right along Baulk Lane. The views from this lane are extensive: on a good day you will be able to see Lincoln Cathedral to the east. Follow the lane to reach a Y-junction. Bear right to follow the footpath sign down a green lane that soon ends in a field. The tower of Laxton Church can be seen in the distance. Yellow waymarkers now lead you around the edges of several fields: go through hedges and over stiles to return to the plaque in Mill Field.

At the plaque, turn left (if you have completed the longer walk) or right (if you are on the shorter walk) to head northwards along a track to reach a road at a bend. Cross the road and continue down the bridleway opposite. After 250 yards you will reach a green lane: turn right and follow the lane back into Laxton. When you reach the main street, maintain direction to return to the car park.

POINTS OF INTEREST:

Laxton – This is England's last open fields' village. Under the open field system, land use needs to be carefully regulated. At Laxton simple three course arable rotation is followed. In any year one field is under winter wheat, the second has a spring crop, such as barley, and the third is left fallow. The fallow field is used for grazing so that the sheep and cattle are providing manure. By 1967 the number of sheep and cattle had declined so the rules were changed to allow a forage crop to be grown and cut. There are no animals in the open fields today.

REFRESHMENTS:

The Dovecote Inn, Laxton.

Walk 6   **BESTWOOD COUNTRY PARK** $2\frac{1}{2}$m (4km)

Maps: OS Sheets Landranger 129; Pathfinder 812.

A short walk through history.

Start: At 556476, the car park at the Bestwood Country Park.

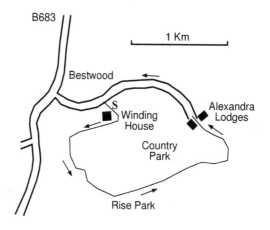

Walk to the **Winding House** of the former Bestwood Colliery, just a few yards from the car park, then follow a cinder track between the winding house and the pump station to reach a sign board by some picnic tables. Turn right and walk uphill: you will soon be overlooking the winding house and have good views into the village of Bestwood.

At a Y-junction, by some seats for those who wish to tarry and enjoy the view, turn left and follow a path which continues to rise, giving even better views. Follow the path towards the houses at Rise Park and another entrance to the Country Park. At the entrance, turn left and follow the signs towards Bigwood.

Walk along the shady lane behind the back gardens of Rise Park. Through the trees on the left you will get a glimpse of a beautifully secluded wooded valley. Soon the gardens, on the right, are replaced by school playing fields: at the next junction go left into the woods, following the path to a T-junction. Turn right and walk along the Woodman's Trail towards Bestwood Lodge Gardens.

Follow the Woodman's Trail to the **Alexandra Lodges**. The path crosses a horse trail: walkers are encouraged not to walk along horse trails and riders are likewise encouraged not to use the footpaths. Take the path to the right, going up steps and around the Lodges to rejoin the Main Drive through the Park. Now follow the Main Drive back to the car park.

POINTS OF INTEREST:

Bestwood Colliery Winding House – This is all that remains of the former colliery. The winding house is being restored by enthusiasts and is open to the public on certain days. The precise dates are given on the notice board.

Alexandra Lodges – This pair of houses straddle the Main Drive to form of an arch.

Bestwood Country Park – The Park was acquired by Nell Gwynne in 1687 and became the seat for the Dukes of St Albans, descendants of Nell Gwynne and King Charles 11. The Park has a network of 20 miles of footpaths through its woodland, grassland and formal gardens set with ponds and lakes, all now given over to conservation and recreation. The wide variety of habitats supports a good range of wildlife. Indeed, the Park is one of the best sites in the Midlands for bird life.

REFRESHMENTS:

None along the route, the nearest being in Hucknall or to the south in Nottingham.

WOLLATON PARK $2^1/_2$m (4km)

Maps: OS Sheets Landranger 129; Pathfinder 833.

Through an historic Nottingham park.

Start: At 530398, the car park inside the entrance to the Park.

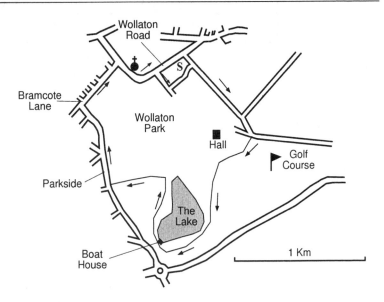

From the car park by Mr Mann's Cafe and Restaurant, take the tree-lined track heading south-westwards through the Park. The track passes a children's playground on the left. Also to the left you can see Nottingham city centre including the Castle, while across the Park to the right you can see **Wollaton Hall**.

Follow the edge of a golf course, first to the right, and then, after a few yards, leftwards. The Hall will now be close by on your right. Continue – with the golf course on your left and the walled gardens of the Hall on your right – to reach a seat, by a bridge over the dried-up moat. Turn left and walk down the long, tree-lined path, heading southwards. The now fenced-off golf course is still on your left.

You are now in the Deer Park and you will get a close view of the red deer that inhabit it as you follow the path to the southern bank of a lake. Follow the path through rhododendrons as it goes around the lake to reach a disused boat house. From the boat house there is a good view of the Hall. Now walk up the western side of the lake to reach a brick bridge across a ditch. This bridge also offers a good view of the hall. Turn left, westwards, and follow a path through a wooden gate, then through bushes and across the Park to reach another gate.

Go through the gate and take the pedestrian path out of the Park into Parkside. Turn right and walk along Parkside to reach Bramcote Lane. Cross Bramcote Lane to explore the small cemetery with its fine rose garden. Now walk along Bramcote Lane to reach the old village of Wollaton, with its old village water pump and shelter in the middle of a traffic island. Turn right and walk along Wollaton Road, passing St Leonard's Church, to reach Wollaton Park again. Turn right to enter the Park and walk back to the start.

POINTS OF INTEREST:

Wollaton Hall – This magnificent Elizabethan Hall was built by Sir Francis Willoughby and completed in 1588. John Thorpe designed the building using styles from the Gothic, Tudor and the Classic periods. Dutch gables crown its four corners. The Hall was purchased by Nottingham Council in 1925 and is now the home of Nottingham's Natural History Museum.

REFRESHMENTS:

The Admiral Rodney, Wollaton Road, Wollaton.
Mr Mann's Cafe and Restaurant, Wollaton Park.

Walk 8   **CHESTERFIELD CANAL**   3m (5km)

Maps: OS Sheets Landranger 120; Pathfinder 745.

A walk along a section of the Chesterfield Canal and then through historic East Retford.

Start: At 726837, the Gate Inn, Clarborough.

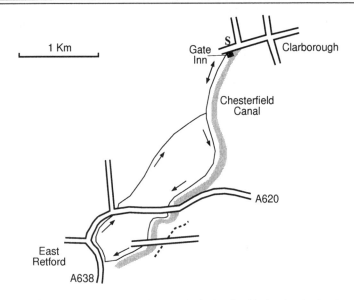

If you use the inn car park, please check with the landlord beforehand. The Gate Inn stands on the west bank of the Chesterfield Canal: walk southwards along the canal tow path, passing fishermen if the season is open. The Canal meanders through open farmland, eventually meeting the Lincoln to Sheffield railway line and the A620 road. Go under the A620 and continue along the canal, now running around the east side of Retford, to reach Grove Mill. Here, turn right and walk into **Retford**.

Cross the A638, with care, and continue into the town centre, passing the museum. From the town centre, head north-eastwards, passing the magnificent Church of St Swithin. Continue along the A620 for 400 yards, then turn left along the A620 diversionary route for high vehicles. After 100 yards, turn right into Bigsby Road.

Follow the road through a quiet housing estate until it makes a sharp right turn. Here, go ahead, through a gate and follow the footpath beyond. This well-used path crosses arable fields and little bridges across ditches, yellow footpath signs guiding you towards a green lane.

Turn right and walk beside a ditch, for 50 yards to reach the green lane. Here, footpath signs direct you back left, over a stile and along a hedge, with the hedge on your left. Follow the path through a couple of hedges as you make your way across fields back to the Chesterfield Canal, reaching it by an outflow. Turn left, cross the outflow and walk along the canal to return to the Gate Inn.

POINTS OF INTEREST:

Retford – Retford is a fine old market town worthy of exploration. When the Great North Road (the A1) was diverted to Retford in 1766 the importance of the town increased dramatically. The market square is dominated by a monument, with an ever burning light, to those who died in the two World Wars. East and West Retford are joined by an iron bridge over the River Idle.

REFRESHMENTS:

The Gate Inn, Clarborough.
There are also opportunities in Retford to suit all tastes and pockets.

BLIDWORTH WOODS   3m (5km)

Maps: OS Sheets Landranger 120; Pathfinder 795.

A walk through part of the ancient Royal Forest of Sherwood.

Start: At 592524, the Forestry Commission car park in Longdale Lane.

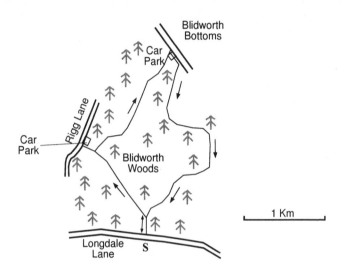

Leave the car park along the broad trail going northwards into Blidworth woods, pausing to read the welcoming notice by a vehicle barrier at a junction of forestry tracks. From the junction, continue northwards for a few yards, then take the footpath going diagonally left (north-westwards). The path is waymarked with blue-topped posts. Follow the path across heathland and then uphill into woodland. At a Y-junction of paths, follow the blue-topped posts to the left, and then to the right. The path ascends to reach a T-junction: go right, continuing to follow the blue-topped posts through mixed woodland. Some of the conifer trees have been felled for timber, young saplings having been planted in these areas for cropping in later years.

You will now reach blue and white posts: follow these uphill to reach the car park and picnic site at Rigg Lane. The car park is quite high and provides good views over the surrounding countryside, particularly to the west. From the car park, follow the blue and white posts gently downhill, heading north-eastwards, back into the mixed woodland of **Blidworth Woods**. The path keeps to the right of a horse-riding trail to reach a junction of forestry tracks. Turn right along a wide forest track, still following the blue and white posts. The track meanders gently downhill: follow the blue and white posts across a wide forest track. The woodland is now silver birch mixed with conifers. Continue to follow the posts to reach the car park and picnic site at Blidworth Bottoms. The toilets marked on some OS map have unfortunately been removed because of vandalism.

A variety of waymarked paths lead out of the car park: take the yellow waymarked bridleway on the east side of Blidworth Woods, a fine route offering views, on the left, across arable farmland to Robin Hood Hill on the horizon. The bridleway ascends a hill: at the top, follow the yellow waymarkers leftwards, following the edge of the wood as it turns eastwards. After 550 yards the path turns right, southwards, and goes back into the woods, taking you between Blidworth Woods and a little oak coppice. You now rejoin the edge of Blidworth Woods and continue southwards, with arable fields on your left. Follow the path as it descends, with excellent views over the farmland to the left.

The edge of Blidworth Woods bends right, then, after another 200 yards, bends back left to continue heading southwards. At this second bend, take the track going almost straight on (heading westwards), rejoining the blue-topped posts after 20 yards. Turn left and follow the blue posts across heathland. Go past a seat provided for weary walkers (and offering delightful views over the surrounding countryside) and continue to follow the blue posts to reach a broad track. Turn left and follow the track back to the welcoming notice board and the start.

POINTS OF INTEREST:

Blidworth Woods – This is a popular recreational spot. The Forestry Commission (now called Forest Enterprise) has provided car parks and picnic sites as well as waymarked walks and horse-riding trails. The woods are at the heart of the ancient Royal Forest of Sherwood and, with the oak trees and open heathland, still have echoes of the ancient Sherwood Forest.

REFRESHMENTS:

None on the walk, though three picnic sites are passed. The nearest are in Blidworth a short distance to the north.

Walk 10   **HAYWOOD OAKS**   3m (5km)

Maps: OS Sheets Landranger 120; Pathfinder 795 and 796.

A fine section of the ancient Royal Forest of Sherwood.

Start: At 605549, the Forestry Commission car park in Haywood
Oaks Lane.

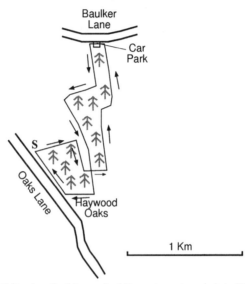

Leave the car park by following the blue and white posts eastwards into **Haywood
Oaks**. Go past the picnic site and continue along the wide and well-used track as it
curves into the mixed, coniferous and deciduous, woodland. You will pass the
occasional gnarled oak as the track narrows into a path. Continue to follow the blue
and white posts to reach a wide riding track. Cross this, but at the next junction turn
right, southwards, still following the blue and white posts as you walk along a broad
track. After 250 yards, turn left, eastwards, following blue signposts along a track to
reach the edge of the woodland.

Turn left and walk, initially, uphill along the side of Haywood Oaks, with views
to the right over arable fields. After 500 yards the boundary of the wood turns right,
eastwards, as do the blue signposts: follow them, and continue to follow them when
they turn left, northwards, after a further 130 yards.

Continue to walk along the edge of the woods, with views to the right across arable farmland to reach Baulker Lane, the Blidworth to Farnsfield road. Turn left and walk along a track, heading away from the road to reach a car park. Now turn left again and follow a bridleway to the vehicle barrier. Go past the barrier and continue to follow the bridleway, which is marked by both blue bridleway and yellow footpath signposts. The tower of Blidworth Church can be seen protruding above the horizon, to your right.

At a junction of forestry tracks, turn right, westwards, to follow the yellow bridleway signposts along the edge of the woods. After about 400 yards the boundary of the woods turns sharp left (south-eastwards). The yellow bridleway signposts follow the edge, and you follow the signposts. Continue along the track as it meanders through mixed woodland, with oak and holly interspersed with coniferous trees. When you reach a broad track, turn right, then turn back left after 10 yards, still following the yellow bridleway signposts.

Blue signposts now reappear: follow the broad track southwards, crossing the path that brought you from the car park. Now follow the blue and white signposts further south and, at a bend in the broad track, follow the blue and white signposts to the right (heading westwards). Follow the footpath to reach Haywood Oaks Lane. From there, turn right and follow the blue and white signposts along a bridleway, heading away from the road to return to the picnic site and car park.

POINTS OF INTEREST:

Haywood Oaks – The wood is named after its large, ancient oak trees. The wood was once part of the Haywood Oaks Manor that was given to the Peverill family by William the Conqueror. The Forestry Commission (now called Forest Enterprise) has provided car parks and a picnic site, as well as waymarked walks and horse-riding trails. These woods are at the heart of the ancient Royal Forest of Sherwood.

REFRESHMENTS:

None on the walk, though there is a picnic sites at the start. The nearest are in Blidworth a short distance to the west.

Walk 11   **WALLINGWELLS WOOD**   3m (5km)

Maps: OS Sheets Landranger 120; Pathfinder 744.

Through a fascinating wood.

Start: At 588839, Carlton in Lindrick Church.

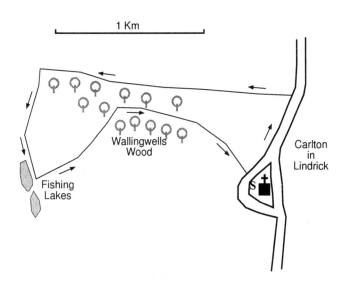

Leave the church by walking north-eastwards along Church Lane to reach the A60. Turn left and walk along the wide pavement beside the main road for 300 yards, then, opposite the Sherwood Ranger Inn, turn left along the signed footpath for Wallingwells.

The footpath starts as an ally between houses, but soon becomes a wide path between the back gardens of houses, on the right, and fields on the left. After 550 yards the path enters Wallingwells Wood. In the spring the ground is flooded with the blue haze of bluebells.

When the path meets a crossing track – about 1,100 yards from the road – turn right for 5 yards, then back left along a signed path. You are now in an area of paddocks and fields, through which the path is both well-marked and bounded on either side by fencing.

Cross a track at Bovellas Kennels and continue westwards, following the footpath sign. Go along an alley between a smallholding, behind the hedge on the left, and fields on the right. Follow the path to reach a track. Turn left (southwards) and follow bridleway signs to reach a junction of tracks in the shape of an inverted Y. Take the stem of the Y, heading south-westwards into the hamlet of Wallingwells. Now look for a bridleway sign by the post box following its direction through a gate into a paddock (heading south-south-east). Go through the gate into an arable field and continue to reach twin lakes which are managed by Wallingwells Angling Club. At the lakes, turn left and follow the bridleway across fields, climbing to Wallingwells Wood. The bridleway is well-used and easy to follow.

At the wood, turn around to enjoy the view across the farmland. Now follow the well-used bridleway as it curves through the wood. The wood is much explored by local children so try to avoid the many side tracks they have created. The path emerges into arable farmland: cross the fields with a hedge on your right, following the path as it passes through a small patch of woodland. Now go through a gate into a grassy field. Ahead is the tower of Carlton Church. Go through a wooden gate and cross a small patch of grass to reach a gap in a stone wall: go through to reach the **Church of St John the Evangelist**.

POINTS OF INTEREST:
Church of St John the Evangelist – There has been a church on this spot for over 1,000 years. The church is mentioned in the Doomsday Book and Saxon work still exists in the tower. The west doorway is Norman, but the top storey and the buttresses reaching to the battlements are 15th-century.

REFRESHMENTS:
The Sherwood Range, Carlton in Lindrick.
The Bluebell Inn, Carlton in Lindrick.

Walk 12   **THIEVES WOOD**   3m (5km)

Maps: OS Sheets Landranger 120; Pathfinder 795.

A short walk through a remnant part of Sherwood Forest.

Start: At 541558, the Forestry Commission car park, Thieves Wood.

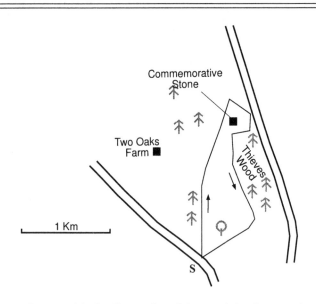

Leave the car park by heading northwards by a rustic barrier to reach a sign indicating a choice of waymarked walks. Go left along a broad lane, following blue and white painted wooden posts. This lane is called the **King's Way**. Follow the lane to the corner boundary of Two Oaks Farm. The white signposts now go along a trail to the right: continue to follow the blue-topped wooden posts, heading northwards through the wood for about 250 yards to reach a junction of tracks.

Turn left, again following the blue-topped posts. After about 250 yards, turn right (north-north-eastwards) and follow the track to reach a clearing by some private houses, at the end of Thieves Wood Lane. Now follow the blue topped posts along another track through the wood, heading south-east towards the A60. The blue topped posts guide you back into the trees, heading southwards and then turning right to follow another track to a picnic site. A short diversion north-westwards from the picnic site will bring you to a **Commemorative Stone**.

Return to the picnic site and head south, and then south-eastwards along the track, now following blue and white posts. The track reaches the boundary of the wood and Campfield Farm: turn right and walk along the boundary track for about 450 yards. Now follow the track as it goes right, back into the woods. Continue along the track to return to the car park.

POINTS OF INTEREST:

The King's Way – This once was the main route joining the castles of Nottingham, Tickhill and Bolsover. It also became the main thoroughfare between Nottingham and Mansfield.

Commemorative Stone – This stone marks the spot the only Egyptian Nightjar known to have visited Britain was shot, on 3 June 1883. The bird was preserved and is now in Mansfield Museum.

REFRESHMENTS:

None on the route, though there is usually a mobile cafe parked in the starting car park. The nearest alternatives are in Ravenhead, a little way to the south-east.

Walk 13   SANSOM WOOD   3m (5km)

Maps: OS Sheets Landranger 120; Pathfinder 795.

A historically interesting short walk.

Start: At 577508, the Burntstump Country Park car park.

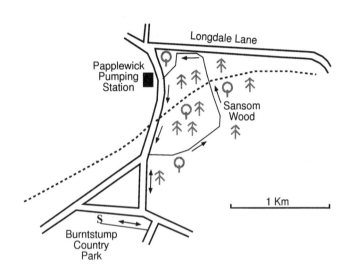

Walk eastwards along the track out of the car park into the Country Park, passing a pond full of aquatic wildlife. Continue along the track, passing a conservation area. The track reaches another: turn left and follow the track towards a road, passing a Victorian church and school built in 1902.

Cross the road, turn left and then, after 50 yards, take the track on the right, following it as it gently descends through woodland. On this section you will get a glimpse of the chimneys of **Papplewick Pumping Station**, to the left. The track emerges on to a country lane at a lay-by for Sansom Wood. Turn right (eastwards) and walk along a broad track into Sansom Wood. At a junction the main track bears left: go with it, then after 250 yards, at another junction, go left again. You are now heading northwards. Cross an austere concrete bridge with iron railings over a railway line, soon after reaching Longdale Lane.

Turn left by the wooden barrier and walk along a pleasant path a few yards to the south of Longdale Lane. After 300 yards you will reach a cross-paths, to the right a wooden barrier and a Robin Hood Way sign pointing across Longdale Lane. Turn left and walk into Sansom Wood, following a narrow, but well-used path. At a Y-junction, go right (south-south-westwards), following a line of telegraph poles. At another cross-paths, turn right and follow a path between deciduous trees, on the right, and conifers on the left. Follow the path to reach a country road close to the Papplewick pumping station.

Turn left and walk along the road to reach a bridge across the railway. Cross the bridge and then, after 50 yards, re-enter Sansom Wood and follow a path that runs parallel to the road to reach the outward route. Now reverse the outward route back to the car park.

POINTS OF INTEREST:

Papplewick Pumping Station – The pumping station is open to the public on most Sunday afternoons between Easter and October. On some Sundays and on Bank Holiday weekends its steam engines are in use.

REFRESHMENTS:

The Burntstump Inn, near the start of the walk.

Walk 14　　　　　　　　**FARNDON**　　　　　　　3m (5km)

Maps: OS Sheets Landranger 120; Pathfinder 796.

Along the banks of the River Trent with good views.

Start: At 768521, the car park opposite the Britannia Inn.

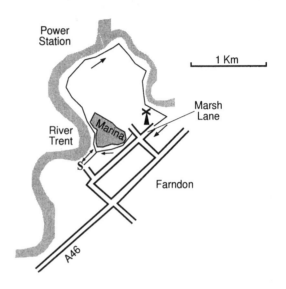

The car park lies beside the River Trent: from it, follow a footpath heading north-eastwards and then northwards across a patch of grassland. In season you will pass members and guests of the Nottinghamshire Anglers Association sat on the banks of the Trent. Go over a footbridge across the entrance to **Farndon Marina**, noticing the sliding mechanism which allows tall boats in and out.

　　Continue walking along the riverbank, with fields on your right. At a junction of paths, continue along the riverbank, now heading north-westwards and passing through open farm land. To the right you will see the chimneys of British Sugar in Newark, a contrast to the fields across the river.

Continue along the riverbank of the Trent, passing the power station at Staythorpe (on the opposite bank). Soon after, at the Newark Dyke weir, a branch of the River Trent goes north. The two branches reunite just north of Newark. Across the river, beyond the fields and a railway line, you will be able to see Kelham Hall.

Continue walking along the riverbank as it meanders its way through an ox-bow, bending back south-eastwards. A stern notice on a gate indicates a private field, the public path continuing along the riverbank beside the field towards the A46 bridge. Go through a gate to reach a converted windmill.

Turn sharp right, go past a metal barrier and walk down a narrow lane. The old windmill is behind the wall on the left, while to the right is a hawthorn hedge. Cross an unmade road and continue along a path, and then an unmade road, heading south-westwards into **Farndon**. The track becomes a tarmac road, Marsh Lane.

At a roundabout, turn right into Walter's Close, a small estate of houses. Now take a signed footpath along a farm track for 100 yards, then turn left along a track, passing Farndon Marina. Follow the path through a group of garages to reach North End. Walk along North End to its junction with Wyke Lane. Now turn right and walk back to the car park.

POINTS OF INTEREST:

Farndon Marina – The Marina was built to cater for the leisure activities of those who enjoy travelling along the River Trent. A wide variety of craft will be seen moored here.

Farndon – Set close to Roman Foss Way, Farndon used to be an important crossing place of the River Trent. Later, a chain ferry – sadly no longer in operation – once brought passengers across the river from Rolleston.

REFRESHMENTS:
The Britannia Inn, Farndon.

Walk 15 **WILFORD** 3m (5km)
Maps: OS Sheets Landranger 129; Pathfinder 833.
Along the banks of the River Trent to Trent Bridge.
Start: At 568379, Main Road, Wilford: please park considerately.

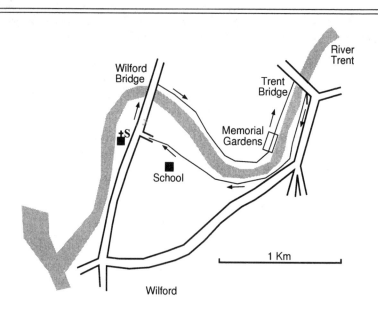

Walk northwards along Main Street to **Wilford Bridge**. Main Street is bounded by embankments so the walker will get a better view by walking on top of either embankment. Cross the River Trent – the bridge gives a good view into the centre of Nottingham City a mere 15 minute walk away – and turn right along Victoria Embankment. By the bridge is a statue of Sir Robert Juckes Clifton Bart MP who died, aged 99, and was the last male of the family.

Walk along Victoria Embankment, a vast, mile long green lawn with a flight of steps leading to the river itself. Anglers, canoeists and rowers all derive great pleasure from this stretch on the river.

Follow the embankment past a suspension bridge over the river. On the left you will pass the **Memorial Gardens**. Above the gates is the inscription 'Virtue is Immortal'.

Go under **Trent Bridge**, looking out for the carved marks in the wall showing the high water marks of various floods between 1852 and 1947. Once under the bridge, turn left, climb up to the road and cross the bridge. As you cross you can see into the terraces of the Nottingham Forest football ground. The buildings around the Nottingham County football ground and the Trent Bridge cricket ground can also be seen from the bridge.

Turn left by the Rushcliffe Civic Centre and walk under the bridge again. Parts of this southern section of Trent Bridge date back to a medieval stone bridge. Now walk southwards along the bank of the Trent, passing close to the County Hall with its distinctive green copper roof. Go past the suspension bridge again, continuing along the riverbanks.

The footpath becomes an alleyway as it passes behind some properties and then emerges on to open ground. Follow the path along the top of an embankment, passing playing fields on the left. The river, on the right, is now bending away to the north. Follow the raised path across open ground, passing the local school and reaching Coronation Avenue as it passes under a disused railway line.

Walk along the top of the bank beside Coronation Avenue. To the right you will see a pond well-known for its wildlife. Follow the path to reach Main Road opposite the Ferry Inn.

POINTS OF INTEREST:
Wilford Bridge – Originally built in 1870 as a toll bridge, the bridge was owned and run by the Clifton family until 1969 when it was taken over by the local council. In 1974 the bridge was closed to motorised traffic and has since been rebuilt for foot and cycle traffic only.
The Memorial Gardens – Designed by Wallis Gordon, the City Engineer, the Gardens are a tribute to all from Nottingham who fell in the two World Wars and, later, in Korea.
Trent Bridge – This has always been an important link between the North and South of England. The first wooden bridge was built over a thousand years ago. This was replaced in medieval times by a stone bridge with a chapel. The present bridge was built in 1870 but has since been extensively modified.

REFRESHMENTS:
The Ferry Inn, Wilford.
The Toll Bridge, Victoria Embankment.

Walk 16   **BAGTHORPE**   3m (5km)

Maps: OS Sheets Landranger 120; Pathfinder 795.
A picturesque walk through D H Lawrence country.
Start: At 474508, Underwood Church.

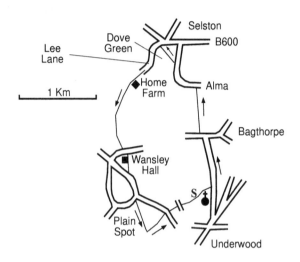

Please park with consideration in Westbourne Road. From the church, walk northwards down Church Lane to reach the sleepy village of Bagthorpe. The road dips to a bridge across a tree-shaded stream, beyond which you will reach a T-junction. Cross and walk up the unmade track almost opposite to reach a sports field. Walk through the sports field to reach a stile. Go over into a paddock and follow a well-used path uphill, through five grassy fields to reach the hamlet of Alma. Just before going through an alley into Alma, look behind for a magnificent view across the valley back to the church at Underwood. Go through the alley and turn left along Inkerman Road. The road bends right by the telephone box: continue along it towards Selston, then take the tarmac footpath on the left, walking between private gardens, on the right, and fields on the left. Cross a stream and walk along an alley between bungalows to reach a road. Cross and walk through the alley opposite to reach an unmade road. Follow the road around to the right to reach Nottingham Road in Dove Green (the B600).

Turn left for 50 yards, then turn left into Lee Lane. At its end, follow a signed footpath on the left along an unmade track. Ahead you can see the spire of Underwood Church. The lane bends right by a stream and continues to Home Farm. Go to the right of the farm, passing between buildings and the stream. Go over a stile and continue along the lane to reach a field gate. Go along the left edge of the arable field beyond, walking beside the hedge and ditch. Go over a metal and concrete bridge across the ditch into a grass field. Follow the well-used footpath through a hedge, then step between a pair of concrete posts into an area of waste land by an oak tree. Now take the path on the left, crossing another ditch over a wooden bridge. Go over a stile on the left and walk up the right side of a grass field. Now cross further grassy fields to reach a lane by Wansley Hall. Go over the stile opposite and cross four grassy fields, using steps out of the last field to reach a lane. Go ahead (south-south-eastwards) along the lane for 100 yards to reach a telephone box and a junction of lanes at Plain Spot. Cross and walk up the unmade bridleway opposite. At its end, go over a stile into a grass field and walk along the hedge on the left, with excellent views to the right into east Derbyshire.

About 550 yards from the road junction you will reach a significant gap in the hedge on the left, and an obvious crossing of footpaths. Turn left along the well-used path to reach a tarmac path. Continue north-eastwards along the path to reach a kissing gate. Beyond, the path ceases to be metalled: follow it through a paddock to reach another kissing gate. Go through and follow an alley between houses and the Hole in the Wall Inn. Cross the road and go along the footpath opposite, between houses, to reach another road. Cross to the footpath opposite, with the spire of **Underwood Church** directly ahead. When you reach Smeath Road, cross into Westbourne Road and walk back to the start of the walk.

POINTS OF INTEREST:
St Michael's and All Angels' Church, Underwood – Colliery winding headstock is set in the churchyard as a tribute to the importance to the village of the former mining industry. Look, also, for the oak shingles on the church spire. As you will have noticed on the walk, the spire dominates the surrounding countryside.

REFRESHMENTS:
The Red Lion, Church Lane, Underwood.
Dixies Arms, Lower Bagthorpe.
The Miner's Arms, Inkerman Road, Alma.
The Hole in the Wall, Underwood.

Walk 17   **COTGRAVE**   4m (6$\frac{1}{2}$km)

Maps: OS Sheets Landranger 129; Pathfinder 834.

Through Cotgrave Forest to Nottingham Airport and along a section of the Grantham Canal.

Start: At 647352, the shopping precinct car park, Cotgrave.

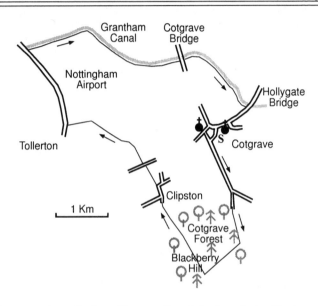

From the car park, walk along Risegate. Turn left along Scrimshire Lane, which becomes Owthorpe Road. Follow the road south-eastwards, uphill out of Cotgrave. When the road turns sharp left, about a mile out of the village, go straight ahead along a bridleway. After about 450 yards you will cross Mill Lane: continue for another 650 yards, then turn right to walk south-westwards through Cotgrave Forest. After about 1,000 yards, turn right again and head north-north-west towards Blackberry Hill.

Leave Cotgrave Forest to enter the gentle arable farmland that is so typical of Nottinghamshire. Walk along Wolds Lane towards the hamlet of Clipston, going through Blackberry Farm to reach a narrow road at a bend. Look out for the Victorian Post Box in the wall. Go ahead, along the road, for 150 yards, then turn first left, at a bend, and, after 25 yards, go right along a marked footpath. Follow the path north-westwards (and downhill) through two fields to reach the Cotgrave/Plumtree road. Cross the road and go into the field opposite. Now maintain direction, walking with a hedge on your right. After about 550 yards you will reach a T-junction with another footpath: turn left and follow a well-marked path across fields, heading towards the small airstrip, known as Nottingham Airport, at Tollerton. The hangers loom ever larger as you approach. The path crosses a small stream and joins a farm track: follow this to reach a road at the outskirts of Tollerton.

Turn right and walk along the road for a mile to reach the **Grantham Canal**, passing the airport entrance and the Tiger Moth Inn. In addition to the aircraft activity the road also offers, just before the canal is reached, good views of the city of Nottingham. The canal is reached at Tollerton Bridge: turn right on to the canal towpath, passing two disused locks and a deserted lock keeper's cottage, relics of a former industrial age. At Cotgrave Bridge there is a car park which is an alternative start for the walk. Continue along the canal towpath, passing another disused lock gate.

At Hollygate Bridge turn right and walk along Holly Lane into the village of Cotgrave, passing the Hollygate light industrial park, and Hollygate Stables and Livery. Holly Lane becomes Bingham Road as the walker gets closer to the village centre: go past the brick Methodist Church and continue to the car park.

POINTS OF INTEREST:

Grantham Canal – The canal is 33 miles long and runs from the River Trent in Nottingham to Earls Field Lane in Grantham. Opened in 1797, the canal allowed the easy shipment of goods between Nottingham and Grantham in Lincolnshire. Its decline started with the opening of the Nottingham to Grantham railway line and it was officially closed in 1929. Two sites along the canal are designated as Sites of Special Scientific Interest because of the aquatic wildlife. The canal is well-stocked with a wide variety of fish including pike, tench, bream and carp.

REFRESHMENTS:
The Manvers Inn, Cotgrave.
The Tiger Moth Inn, Nottingham Airport.

Walks 18 & 19   **EAST BRIDGFORD**   4m (6$\frac{1}{2}$km)
or 6m (10km)

Maps: OS Sheets Landranger 129; Pathfinder 813.

Along the River Trent, returning through gentile farmland with extensive views.

Start: At 694429, the car park in East Bridgford.

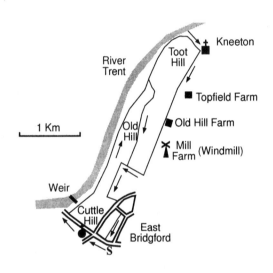

Leave the car park and turn left to walk along Main Street, heading towards St Peter's Church. At the crossroads, go straight across and walk down Trent Lane, heading towards the River Trent. After 50 yards, turn left along a path, keeping above the road, which has no footpath. After a further 500 yards the path re-emerges on to the road: cross and take the left of two footpaths, following it past a marina and through a gate to reach the east bank of the **River Trent** close to a weir. On the far bank is Gunthorpe Lock. At this point the path can, in certain seasons become overgrown and soggy, but perseverance will bring you to easier walking on a broad bridleway. Continue along the Trent's bank. The landscape here is characterised by two major features. The first is the steep wooded cliffs made up of Red Mercia Mudstone, with layers of white gypsum. The second is the flat, open riverside pastures that traditionally relied on regular flooding to maintain their fertility. As the meadow broadens, keep to the base of the cliffs, passing Watson's Piece.

The shorter walk bears right here, going up Toot Hill. Walk up the narrow bridleway, with grand views of the river. The track curves back towards East Bridgford and broadens as it gets higher. Here it offers excellent views over Nottinghamshire. Follow the track to reach a T- junction. Turn right, here, rejoining the longer walk.

From Watson's Piece the longer route crosses a stile and continues beside a row of willows, heading northwards across a broad meadow. Cross another stile and continue along the broad meadow banks of the Trent. A vague track will soon become apparent on the right: follow this track to a gate by woodland. Go over a stile and go up the track beyond to reach the village of Kneeton by St Helen's Church. Turn right at the church, heading south-west along a lane. The lane becomes a track and then goes through a gate into fields. Maintain direction beside a hedge, heading towards the converted windmill of Mill Farm. The views across the Trent Valley are excellent here. Go through a hedge and maintain direction. Near Topfield Farm the path crosses fields instead of going along their edges, but the route is well used and easy to follow. Cross a track at Old Hill Farm and continue across fields, passing to the east of the converted windmill at Mill Farm. The path now reaches a track: turn right along the track for 300 yards, heading towards the River Trent and rejoining the shorter walk.

Continue north-eastwards along the track for a further 130 yards, then turn left along a footpath that follows the edge of a field, walking with a hedge on your left. The reassuring hedge stops: maintain direction for a further 280 yards to where the path stops in the middle of a field. Turn left and walk across the field (the way is usually well worn) to reach a road. Turn right along the road, then, after 100 yards, turn left along Cherry Holt Lane. Follow the lane for 130 yards, then turn right along a footpath, following it to Main Street, East Bridgford. Turn left to return to the car park.

POINTS OF INTEREST:
River Trent – At all times of the year the abundant wildlife will keep walkers entertained. Herons are common as are ducks and geese, and anglers will be pleased to inform you about the nature (and the size) of their catch.

REFRESHMENTS:
The Reindeer Inn, Kneeton Road, East Bridgford.

Walk 20   OSSINGTON   4m (6km)

Maps: OS Sheets Landranger 120; Pathfinder 780.
A fine walk through woods and across fields.
Start: At 759651, Holy Rood Church, Ossington.

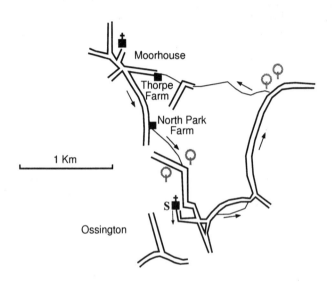

The walk starts at the sandstone **Holy Rood Church** in the hamlet of Ossington. Walk eastwards along the church drive to reach its junction with a lane. Go straight across, stepping over a low barrier and continuing along a bridleway. Follow the bridleway to reach a road by Gardeners Cottage. Continue eastwards for 150 yards, then turn right at a footpath sign. The path takes you around a house, past dog kennels, and into a strip of woodland. Maintain direction along the wooded green lane to reach a road by a bend. Turn right, and then almost immediately left along a bridleway.

     Head northwards along the bridleway, passing through typical East Midlands farmland with views across the A1 trunk road to Sutton on Trent and Weston. When the bridleway reaches a patch of woodland, turn left and walk along the edge of the wood to reach a hedge. Turn left again to walk beside the hedge to reach another patch of woodland. Now follow blue bridleway signs through the wood, following a wide and obvious path. Leave the wood by crossing a ditch, then follow a hedge to reach a broad band of green swath. Here, the bridleway goes right, heading towards the A1. Do not follow it: instead, follow the yellow arrow waymarkers diagonally across a field to reach the corner of a hedge and the end of a farm track. Walk down the track until it goes off to the left, then cross another field to reach a stile on the opposite side. Cross the stile and the grassy field beyond to reach a track by Thorpe Farm.

Follow the track to the small community of Moorhouse. To the right you will see the hamlet's small church. The track reaches a road: to visit the church turn right, otherwise turn left along the road, heading south towards Ossington. When you reach North Park Farm, take the signed footpath on the left, heading south-east across a field towards the wood in the distance. If the footpath has been ploughed you should aim at the pair of trees that can be seen in the middle of the field. Cross a ditch by way of a wide bridge and maintain direction to reach the corner of the wood.

Yellow arrows now lead you through the wood: continue along a wide track to reach the drive to Ossington Church.

POINTS OF INTEREST:

Holy Rood Church, Ossington – Built of sandstone, this church has a unique classical style. It has a delightful domed tower and round-headed windows.

REFRESHMENTS:

There are none available in either Ossington or Moorhouse. The closest are in Norwell, to the south, or in Laxton, to the west.

Walk 21   **SOUTH SCARLE**   4m (6km)

Maps: OS Sheets Landranger 121; Pathfinder 781.

There are excellent views on this walk to a quaint village.

Start: At 832624, Low Street, Collingham.

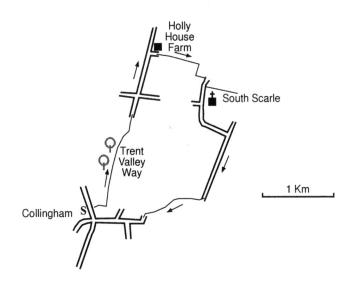

From the start, turn right along the A1133 and follow it for 100 yards, then take the footpath on the right. Head eastwards along the path, which is part of the Trent Valley Way. Follow the path along the edge of a field, passing the backs of several houses, and a school. When the path goes through a hedge into another field, turn left and walk northwards still following the waymarkers for the Trent Valley Way.

    The path continues through several hedges and then through a small patch of woodland. Beyond the woodland, continue along the Trent Valley Way to reach a track. Continue straight ahead, along the track, to reach a road opposite Lodge Farm. This road connects Besthorpe with South Scarle.

Cross the road and continue along the lane opposite, heading north towards Holly House Farm. Turn right at the Folly Farm Pets Hotel, walking along the driveway for a few yards, then crossing a fence and heading eastwards along the line of the fence. Cross a field aiming at the solitary rowan in the hedge in the distance. The hedge marks a corner of a field: follow the hedge in front, which was previously hidden, heading east-south-east to reach a T-junction of footpaths. Turn right and follow a path with yellow waymarkers towards South Scarle.

Follow the path past a farm, on the right, with a stone built dovecote, and, on the left, a wall-mounted post box before reaching St Helena's Church. Continue along Main Street, South Scarle. The road bends left and then back right, finally heading south-westwards. Lincolnshire is now only 500 yards away to your left. Continue along the road, which soon becomes a bridleway.

Follow the track to reach a hedge and a choice of footpaths. Bear right, westwards, cross a wooden bridge and walk along the edge of several fields. The path follows a ditch and then broadens into a farm track: continue along it to reach **Collingham** at a bend in a road. Go straight ahead (westwards) along the road to reach the A1133. Low Street is opposite.

POINTS OF INTEREST:
Collingham – This was originally a Saxon settlement that developed into North and South Collingham. A Saxon Cross still stands at the northern end of the village. The current combined village was amalgamated under one Parish Council in 1974. The villages were formerly thriving communities drawing business from the River Trent. Osier beds, used for basket making by the villagers, have disappeared since the river was dredged and the flood banks were built.

REFRESHMENTS:
There are several possibilities in Collingham.

Walk 22　　　　　　**WELLOW PARK**　　　　　　4m (6km)

Maps: OS Sheets Landranger 120; Pathfinder 780.
Fine walking through beautiful woodland.
Start: At 668665, Wellow Pond car park.

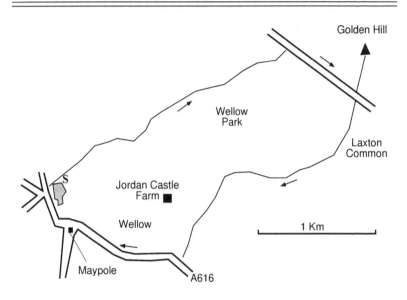

Take the footpath to the north of the pond, heading eastwards along it to reach a track. Continue north-eastwards along the track to reach a Y-junction. Here, bear right, following the yellow arrows into Wellow Park. The Forestry Commission now manage the Park and maintains the footpaths running through it.

At the end of the track you will come out into a meadow: continue along the track to reach the country lane connecting Ollerton with Laxton. Turn right and walk uphill beside the Park for $^1/_2$ mile to reach a track, to the left, leading to the radio mast and trig. point on Golden Hill. The short, 400 yard, detour to the trig. point is well worth the effort. If you do make the detour, return to this point as the route turns right off the road, following a track across Laxton Common and back to Wellow Park. Follow a broad bridleway through the Park, going through woodland with fields visible through the trees to either side.

46

Leave Wellow Park through a gate and turn left along a broad open track. Follow the track across several fields. When the track turns right to Jordan Castle Farm, continue straight on along a path, following it though a narrow strip of woodland and then along the side of a field to reach the A616.

Turn right and, with great care, follow the road back into **Wellow**. Go past the village **Pinfold**. Continue along the main road to return to the car park.

POINTS OF INTEREST:

Wellow – Wellow is a conservation village. The permanent maypole is well known and attracts visitors from far and wide for the traditional crowning of the May Queen, a ceremony which goes back centuries.

Wellow Pinfold – The Pinfold was built in 1842: stray stock was kept here until the owners were found. The owners were required to pay a fine to retrieve their stock.

REFRESHMENTS:
The Durham Ox, Wellow.
The Olde Red Lion, Wellow.

Walk 23   **TILN**   4m (7km)

Maps: OS Sheets Landranger 120; Pathfinder 745.

A walk to a small hamlet in the River Idle valley.

Start: At 723853, the lay-by on the B1403 just north of Hayton.

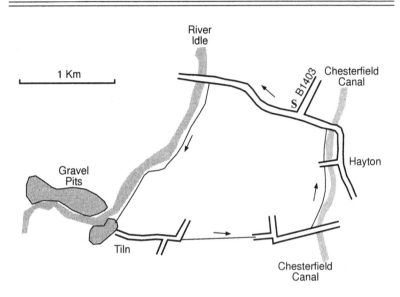

There is limited car parking in the lay-by near the sharp right-hand bend on the B1403 about a mile from the centre of Hayton. From the lay-by walk westwards along the bridleway which leaves the road at the bend. The bridleway is known as Chain Bridge Lane. The valley of the **River Idle** is very flat and interlaced with irrigation ditches and dikes. There are good views of this system from the track.

At the River Idle a very severe concrete bridge carries Chain Bridge Lane across the water. Do not cross the bridge: instead, turn left and walk along the river's eastern bank. The raised bank of the river gives good views across the valley, eastwards to Hayton and Clarborough, and westwards to Lound and Sutton. This stretch of the river is used by the Derbyshire County Angling Club, despite being many miles from the county. The sand and gravel pits on the western side of the river attract many different species of waterfowl. The walker may even see the occasional water vole (as water rats are properly called).

After 1$^{1}/_{4}$ miles you will reach a gate and stile beside a farmhouse: go over or through to reach the hamlet of Tiln. The track now becomes a metalled road: continue along the road for a few yards, then turn left, opposite a row of cottages, towards an open yard. Go into the yard beside a white cottage. At the other side of the yard you will find a track heading east, towards Hayton: take this.

Initially the track is beside a corrugated fence erected to stop the wind invading the garden of the white cottage. It then crosses the Idle valley, passing between arable fields, going through hedges and across the occasional ditch. One ditch is crossed by a wooden bridge. Finally, a yellow footpath sign directs you straight across an arable field to a green lane. Maintain direction along the green lane, walking between tall hedges and soon reaching a T-junction. Turn right. After 50 yards the lane turns sharp left: continue along it to reach Bridge No. 63 over the Chesterfield Canal.

Do not cross the bridge: instead, turn left and follow the towpath along the western bank of the canal, passing Cartwheel Cottage, on the left, and some moored narrow boats, on the water. Go underneath two bridges (Nos. 64 and 65), continuing to Bridge No. 66, and the B1403, by the Boat Inn. Go under the bridge and turn left to reach the road. Now either turn right for refreshments at the Boat Inn, or turn right and, with care, follow the road back to the start.

POINTS OF INTEREST:
River Idle – The river and the surrounding flooded gravel pits are home to over 100 species of birds, including waterfowl such as ducks, geese and swans.

REFRESHMENTS:
The Boat Inn, Hayton.

Walk 24   **SHIREOAKS**   4m (6km)

Maps: OS Sheets Landranger 120; Pathfinder 762 and 744.
A walk across typical North Midlands farmland.
Start: At 551807, Shireoaks Park.

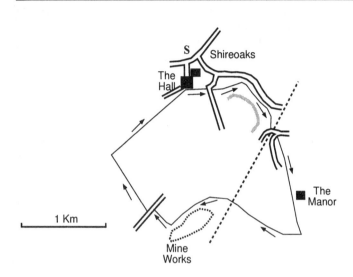

Take the track between the upper and lower lakes. The lakes are stocked with fish that attract fishermen and wildfowl alike. The path goes around to the south of a derelict hall, then crosses the end of what looks to be a canal. Now follow footpath signs through a gate and head eastwards. Go around the outside of a walled garden, with fields on the right, continuing to reach a tarmac drive: follow this to reach a road.

Cross the road and continue along the bridleway opposite, walking with a hedge on your left, and open fields on your right. Cross a stone bridge over the River Ryton to reach a road. Turn right along the road, passing a sports ground. Yellow footpath signs now direct you between the sports ground buildings and a private house: follow the path round the garden of the house to return to the River Ryton. Go over a stile and head south-eastwards across a narrow field between the river and the Chesterfield

Canal. The well-used path crosses the field by a telegraph pole and continues along the hedge to reach woodland. It is possible to climb to the banks of the canal and walk along the canal for 100 yards. Turn right and follow the woodland edge to reach a stile.

Go over the stile and follow the footpath beyond to reach a road by a railway embankment. Turn left along the road, going under the railway line, and then turning right at Haggonfields Farm to go along a bridleway signed for Mansfield Road. Follow the track as it bends left, away from the railway line. On the left you will pass the Lady Lee Quarry Nature Reserve. The track now crosses the River Ryton and then passes **Manor Lodge**. As the track continues across high farmland it affords excellent views.

About 250 yards beyond the Manor Lodge a path crosses the track: turn right and follow the path across fields, heading west towards mine works. This very clear path passes from field to field through hedges and across ditches to reach the railway line. Go under the railway and continue between a field and the Baker Refractory Streetley works: yellow arrows direct you through a wooded area circumventing the works. Eventually the path emerges from the wood on to a service road for the works: follow the service road to reach a lane.

Turn left, but after 50 yards, turn right and follow a footpath, heading north-westwards along the edge of a field. Go through a hedge and cross another field to reach a stile. Go over on to a track and turn right along it. When the track starts to bend to the left, go straight on along a bridleway. Ahead you can see the Hall at Shireoaks, while to the right, across the fields, is Manor Lodge. Light aircraft from Netherthorpe Airfield will often be heard and seen overhead.

Go through a gate and cross an arable field to reach another gate. Go through and follow a path back to the start of the walk.

POINTS OF INTEREST:
Manor Lodge – Now a hotel, the Lodge was built in 1593. As you will note on the walk, this magnificent tall building stands as a landmark above the surrounding fields.

REFRESHMENTS:
The Hewett Arms, Shireoaks Park.

Walk 25 **PLEASLEY VALE** 4m (6km)
Maps: OS Sheets Landranger 120; Pathfinder 779.
A walk with historical interest.
Start: At 508648, the Pleasley Vale car park.

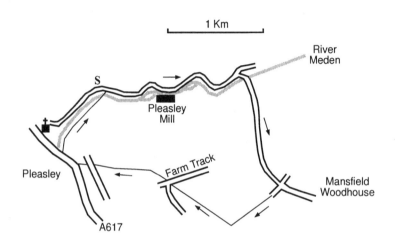

Leave the eastern side of the car park, following the Creswell Archaeological Way footpath to enter a shady wooded area beside the River Meden. Follow the path through the woods to reach a fence. Here, footpath signs indicate ways both left and right: turn right and descend into the Meden Valley. The remains of the manager's house of the former **Pleasley Mill** can be seen from the valley path. Cross the old mill's weir and then cross a bridge over the River Meden. Upstream can be seen the remains of the old mill chimney. Climb the bank to reach a dismantled railway line and turn left.

Walk along the cinder track that was once the railway trackbed, with trees and shrubs providing dappled shade in hot summer sunshine. The track passes under a stone bridge, a relic of when Pleasley Mill was an active commercial site. The trees and shrubs begin to thin out as you continue along the track. Soon, to the right, fields can be seen, and before long there are fields on both sides of the track. Go through a kissing gate to reach a country road. Turn right and walk along the road towards Mansfield Woodhouse. At the crossroads, turn right into Northfield Lane.

Follow Northfield Lane to its end, then continue south-westwards along an 'alleyway' between two hedgerows. As the footpath gently climbs you will be greeted by glorious views across the surrounding fields. Continue to the top of the hill where there is a choice of routes.

Turn right and take the path that heads across fields, going through hedges. The remains of **Pleasley Mine** can be clearly seen across the main A617, the trunk road connecting Mansfield with the M1 motorway. Follow the path to reach a farm track where it makes a sharp turn. Cross the track and walk into a field. Cross the field, walking with a hedgerow on your left, to reach a significant gap filled by a fence.

Cross the stile over the fence to reach two paths. Take the path on the right, walking with a hedgerow on your right and heading west towards Pleasley and the A617. Follow the path as it passes from one field to another through a gap in the hedge, then cross the next field along a well-used footpath that reaches a track. Cross the track and another field to reach a hedge. The path now descends a steep and wooded bank to reach the pavement beside the A617.

Turn right and walk along the pavement for about 150 yards to reach a track on the right, by the River Meden. Go right, then left to walk along the bank of the river. Cross a bridge over the river and continue along the opposite bank to return to the car park.

POINTS OF INTEREST:
Pleasley Mill – Initially this was an iron forge. In 1784 it was converted into a cotton thread mill and then, in the 1890s, it started producing finished cotton garments.
Pleasley Mine – Now a ruin, this mine is the subject of a heritage and regeneration project. The surviving chimney and winding towers can be seen from many parts of the walk.

REFRESHMENTS:
None along the route, the nearest being in Pleasley.

Walk 26   **BOAR HILL**   4m (6km)

Maps: OS Sheets Landranger 120; Pathfinder 795.

An interesting short walk through typical North Midlands scenery.

Start: At 490558, St Wilfrid's Church, Kirkby-in-Ashfield.

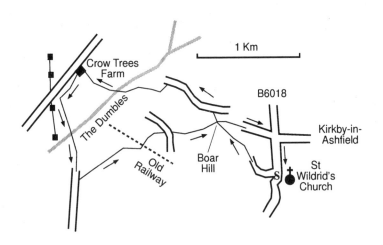

Start from the church car park, crossing the B6018, with care, to reach a stone water trough by the entrance to Manor House Court. Walk along Manor House Court, a small housing estate, to its end, then take a footpath on the left, going between fences to reach fields. Turn right along a track and follow it behind more houses. The track crosses **Boar Hill**. After about 150 yards the track ends: continue along the footpath, heading north-westwards across fields, walking with a hedge on your right (beyond which are playing fields). Cross arable fields along this well-used and distinct path, going through hedges between the fields and finally reaching a track which is followed to a lane.

Turn left and follow the lane as it gently descends. Ahead there are good views into Derbyshire. When you reach a pair of gate posts marking the entrance to private property, a footpath goes off left along a wide lane: follow this lane, which is bounded by tall hedges, following yellow arrow waymarkers into deciduous woodland by a stream called The Dumbels. At the bottom of the valley, cross a bridge over the stream and gently climb the other side of the valley, still following the yellow arrow waymarkers through the trees.

You emerge from the woodland into an arable field with a hedgerow on your right: continue along the path to reach a country lane by Crow Trees Farm. Turn left along the lane for 450 yards. There are a number of footpaths leaving the road on your left side: take the one beneath the power lines marked with a public bridleway sign. Follow the track south-eastwards, passing between arable fields marked by their use as there is no hedge at first. The spire of St Wilfrid's Church can be seen on the horizon.

The path re-joins The Dumbels and crosses it by a wooden bridge. Follow a lane uphill through a wooded area: when the trees cease the lane is still bounded by hedgerows as it passes through fields. As you reach the top of the hill you will be greeted by excellent views all round. Go through a gate by a farmhouse, then turn left over a stile and follow a path north-eastwards, at first between fields and then across fields, heading towards a dismantled railway (though all signs of the trains have long since gone).

Cross the old railway and follow the yellow arrow waymarkers across arable fields to reach a farm track. The yellow arrows now lead you to the right, along the track, for a few yards to reach a gate. Turn left and follow the well-marked path beyond through fields, reclimbing Boar Hill. Cross the path used at the beginning of the walk and head for a tall hedge surrounding the playing fields. Walk eastwards beside the hedge to reach a lane. Follow the lane to reach a footpath on the right. Go through the narrow gate into the playing fields (Titchfield Park). Turn left and walk to the entrance of the playing fields to reach the B6018. Turn right and follow the road back to the church.

POINTS OF INTEREST:
Boar Hill – The hill offers excellent views into east Derbyshire.

REFRESHMENTS:
The Duke of Wellington, Kirkby-in-Ashfield.

Walk 27   BESTWOOD AND MILL LAKES   4m (7km)

Maps: OS Sheets Landranger 129; Pathfinder 812.

A walk through history.

Start: At 556476, the car park at the Bestwood Country Park.

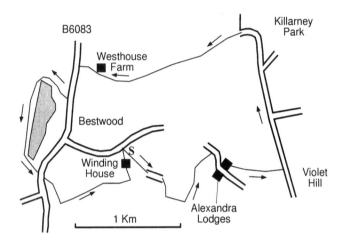

Walk to the **Winding House** of the former Bestwood Colliery, just a few yards from the car park, then follow a cinder track between the winding house and the pump station to reach a sign board by some picnic tables. Follow the sign for Alexandra Lodges. The broad track leads up a valley with grassy fields on the right and scrub land on the left, going into deciduous woodland and winding gently uphill to join the Woodman's Trail. Follow the Trail to the edge of the woods. The path now re-enters the woodland and passes a children's playing area and a toilet block before meeting the Main Drive. Turn right to the Alexandra Lodges, a pair of houses which form an arch straddling the Main Drive. Take the rising Colliers Path left of the Lodges going through woodland to reach Violet Hill and an unmade lane. Turn left and walk towards Killarney Park, an estate of prefabricated homes. To the right you can see the tower of Severn-Trent's Bestwood Pumping Station.

At Killarney Park, turn left along Knightwood Drive. At its end, go through a metal gate into woodland, passing a BT microwave tower and following the well-used path to emerge into an arable field. Follow the path beside the hedgerow on the right, descending to Westhouse Farm. At the bottom of the field, follow a farm track to the left. Go through a large gap in the hedge on the right and follow the track as it bends right to reach the farm. Walk through the farmyard and along the metalled driveway to reach the B683. Turn left and walk towards Bestwood village. Turn right opposite The Spinney to follow a bridleway signed for **Mill Lakes** and Hucknall. Cross the River Leen and turn left into the Mill Lakes Country Park. Walk along the western side of the lakes, which are home to a variety of waterfowl including Brent geese, swans and a variety of ducks. Cross the River Leen again, leaving the park by a stepped path down to the B683.

Cross the B683, with care, and climb the stepped path on the other side on to an embankment. Go past a wooden barrier and walk along the scrub-lined track to meet another track coming in from the left (at an inverted Y). Turn left and follow the well-used track around the Joy Mining and Engineering Works. Go past another wooden barrier to return into **Bestwood Country Park**. At a junction of paths, turn left to walk along the prepared track back to the winding house, the top of which can just be seen over the near horizon.

POINTS OF INTEREST:

Bestwood Colliery Winding House – This is all that remains of the former colliery. The winding house is being restored by enthusiasts and is open to the public on certain days. The precise dates are given on the notice board.

Bestwood Country Park – The Park was acquired by Nell Gwynne in 1687 and became the seat for the Dukes of St Albans, descendants of Nell Gwynne and King Charles II. The Park has a network of 20 miles of footpaths through its woodland, grassland and formal gardens set with ponds and lakes, all now given over to conservation and recreation. The wide variety of habitats supports a good range of wildlife. Indeed, the Park is one of the best sites in the Midlands for bird life.

Mill Lakes – Before the arrival of the colliery the lakes supplied power to two cotton mills, Forge Mill, built on the site of an old iron works, and Middle Mill. The mills have long since gone, but the lakes remain, providing a habitat for waterfowl.

REFRESHMENTS:

None along the route, the nearest being in Hucknall or to the south in Nottingham.

Maps: OS Sheets Landranger 129; Pathfinder 853.
Two fine walks along the Soar valley.
Start: At 504233, the car park in Zouch.

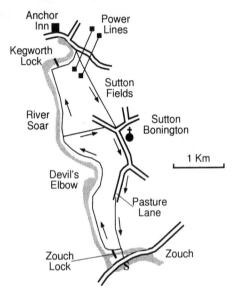

The car park is on the A6006 just to the west of the Rose and Crown Inn in Zouch.
From it, cross the road to the footpath opposite and follow it across a grassy field to
reach a humpback bridge over the River Soar. Cross, turn left and walk along the
riverbank to Zouch Lock, passing numerous narrow boats moored by the bank.
Continue along the riverbank path, passing the lock gates. When the river makes a
sharp right (northward) turn right. To the left, along a branch of the river, you will see
the headquarters of the local rowing club. Continue along the riverbank, crossing
stiles between the fields: this section of the Soar, all the way to its junction with the
River Trent at Ratcliffe, is the boundary between Nottinghamshire and Leicestershire.
As the path passes an island you leave fields for wooded scrub, though the path remains

close to the river. Fields replace the scrub after the river passes the Devils Elbow. Continue to a bend in the river, frustratingly opposite an inn with no bridge. A few yards beyond the bend a footpath goes right (eastwards) to Sutton Bonington.

The shorter walk follows the footpath across fields to reach Soar Lane where the longer route is rejoined.

The longer route continues along the riverbank towards Kegworth. You are now walking beneath the flight path of aircraft landing at the East Midlands Airport. Across the river you will see the beautiful house and grounds of Kegworth Lodge. By the weir an island has been designated as a bird sanctuary, while Kegworth Deep Lock is the next point of interest. Continue along the river bank to reach a country lane. Those wanting refreshments should turn left here, crossing the river and continuing for 200 yards to reach the Anchor Inn. The route makes an about turn, heading south-eastwards to pass under the power lines from the Ratcliffe on Soar Power Station. Cross a stile and follow a well-used and well-marked path through arable fields. Eventually the path goes through a metal kissing gate, with a pond to the right, into a wooded area. At this point the path becomes quite narrow as it squeezes between a hedge and a wire fence. Cross a track and go through another metal kissing gate into a paddock. Ahead now can be seen the spire of St Michael's Church in Sutton Bonington. Follow the path to emerge into Soar Lane near a brick and timber cottage, rejoining the shorter route.

Go south-eastwards along Soar Lane to reach Main Street, **Sutton Bonington**. Go past St Michael's Church and continue along Main Street to reach Pasture Lane, near the Kings Head Inn. Bear left along quiet Pasture Lane, following it to its end. Continue along a track beside fields. The track becomes a path: follow the signs to reach the bridge over the River Soar crossed at the start of the walk. Now reverse the first few yards of the walk to return to the start.

POINTS OF INTEREST:

Sutton Bonington – This long and straggling village is a combination of the former villages of Sutton and Bonington, hence the two churches, rectories (one now a private house) and chapels. The Hall is a fine Queen Anne mansion. The village is also home to Nottingham University's School of Agriculture.

REFRESHMENTS:
The Anchor Inn, Kegworth.
The Kings Head, Sutton Bonington.
The Rose and Crown, Zouch.

Walk 30   WYSALL TO WILLOUGHBY ON THE WOLDS   4m (6km)
Maps: OS Sheets Landranger 129; Pathfinder 854.
Beautiful scenery linking two interesting villages.
Start: At 604271, Holy Trinity Church, Wysall.

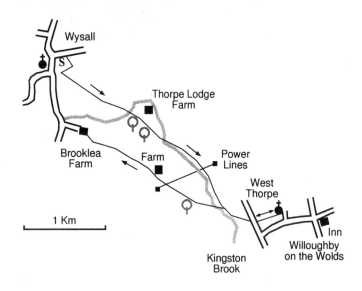

Parking – with care and consideration – is available along Main Street, Wysall. Opposite the church there is a footpath sign pointing down a jitty beside the Village Hall: follow this, walking eastwards down the jitty into a children's play area. Cross the play area to reach a stile. Cross and follow yellow arrows over further stiles and grassy fields to reach the infant Kingston Brook. This river starts life near to Six Hills, in Leicestershire.

Cross Kingston Brook by stiles and bridge in a small wooded area and then go left, following the edge of a field through several changes of direction. Yellow arrows now guide you between Thorpe Lodge Farm and a large wood. Go uphill across an arable field – if the field has been ploughed start by aiming at a telegraph pole – then go over a rickety stile into a field. Follow the hedge on the left for 5 yards to reach a bridge. Cross the bridge (over Kingston Brook again). Turn right and follow the edge of the field to reach a lane at West Thorpe. Cross the lane and then cross several grassy meadows, following yellow arrows towards the village of Willoughby.

Cross the Wysall road to reach another footpath, following it through several grassy meadows on the way to St Mary and All Saints' Church. Turn right and walk down Church Lane into **Willoughby-on-the-Wolds**. Turn left and walk along Main Street. At the crossroads, go straight over and continue along Main Street. Refreshments are available at The Three Horseshoes Inn.

Now retrace your steps to West Thorpe and follow the Midshires Way into a grassy field. Go over a double stile into a second grassy field and cross to a brick bridge over Kingston Brook. Cross the bridge into another grassy field and follow the yellow arrows across several fields towards a small triangular patch of woodland.

Go through a gate and walk along the edge of the field beyond, with the wood on your left. At the end of the wood, the point of the triangle, go through a gap in a hedge between two fields, and turn right. Walk along the boundary hedge, beneath a line of pylons, to reach another wood. Follow the eastern edge of the wood and then go over a stile into a grass field. Follow the telegraph poles across this field, passing to the left of a farmhouse. Cross a stile into a small scrapyard and continue to follow the telegraph poles through scrub to reach a stile. Go over into a grassy field.

Yellow arrows direct you across and around the field to reach Brooklea Farm. Wysall Church can be clearly seen. Now follow tall, yellow-topped posts around the farm to reach its drive. Walk along the drive to reach a road. Turn right and walk along this quiet road back into the village of Wysall.

POINTS OF INTEREST:

Willoughby-on-the-Wolds – In the 13th century the village was home to Ralph Bugge. His son changed the family name to Willoughby. This family later produced Sir Richard Willoughby, a famous Lord Chief Justice. Willoughby was the site of the last battle in Nottinghamshire, during the Civil War, when the Royalists were finally defeated.

REFRESHMENTS:

The Plough Inn, Keyworth Road, Wysall.
The Tress Horseshoes Inn, Main Street, Willoughby-on-the-Wolds.

Walks 31 & 32   **TOLLERTON**   4m (6$^1/_2$km)
or 8m (12km)

Maps: OS Sheets Landranger 129; Pathfinder 833 and 834.
Two walks through beautiful country to the south of Nottingham.
Start: At 589358, the Rushcliffe Leisure Centre.

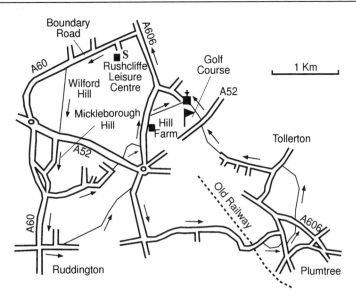

Leave the Centre's main entrance and turn left along Boundary Road to reach the A60 (Loughborough Road). Turn left along this busy road for 100 yards, then turn left to follow a bridleway along the edge of a cemetery, ascending Wilford Hill. At the top, continue along the narrowing bridleway to reach the A52. Cross the dual carriageway, with care, and go through the hedge opposite. Go along Old Road, which ascends Mickleborough Hill, to its end, then turn right along a path beside ' Silva' and descend to the entrance of Ruddington Hall. Turn left along the road to reach the A60 again.

   The shorter walk now turns left, to follow a bridleway, with Ruddington Hall to the left. When the track turns sharp left continue ahead to reach the A52. Cross, again with care, into Weatcroft's Garden Centre. Follow the path signs through the Centre to the A606. Cross, with care, and turn left to reach Hill Farm Court. Turn right and walk through the estate to reach a farm gate. Turn left over a stile and follow a hedge to a disused railway and bridge. Cross the bridge into Edwalton Golf Course. Follow the path signs towards Holy Rood Church to reach Village Street and the longer route.

The longer route goes south along the A60. Turn left at the traffic lights into Flawforth Lane and follow to reach a signed stile on the left just beyond Silverdale Farm. Go over and follow the yellow arrows to a wooded area. Continue eastwards to the end of the wooded area, then turn left to cross a bridge. Walk left around the field edge, then cross a bridge and turn right, crossing a field to reach a stile on to a lane. Turn right along the lane for 750 yards to reach a lay-by. On the left is the site of the former **Flawford Church of St Peter.** A path goes around two sides of the site and then follows a farm track eastwards. The track becomes a green lane, goes beneath a disused railway and then bends right. At a left bend, go over a stile on the right into a field and follow the hedge on the left into the village of Plumtree. Cross Main Street and take the path opposite, beside 'Hill Fields'. Cross a field to a double stile. Do not cross: instead, turn left and walk to the corner of the field and another stile. Go over the stile turn left to reach the A606. Cross, with care, go through the opposite hedge and follow a path diagonally across a field. Cross a stile and a field to another stile. Cross and follow the field edge to Tollerton Lane. Turn left for 150 yards to reach Burnside Grove, following it to a roundabout. Go right into Lothian Road and, at its end, turn left along a track beside a children's play area. Turn right and follow a hedge to its end, then cross a field to reach a hedge and ditch. Cross a bridge and walk beside a hedge. When the hedge goes sharp right, continue across the field to reach a gate. Go through and descend steps to the A52. Cross, with care, and turn right, soon reaching a signed path, using steps to reach a patch of rough scrub. Follow the path through the scrub on to Edwalton Golf Course. Follow the path signs across the golf course to Holy Rood Church. A gate on the right of the church leads to Village Street, where the shorter route is rejoined.

Walk along Village Street to reach Melton Road. Turn right and follow Melton Road to the traffic lights at Boundary Road. Turn left and walk back to the Rushcliffe Leisure Centre.

POINTS OF INTEREST:

Flawford Church of St Peter – On this site there once stood a Saxon church built about AD800. The ground is marked out with the foundations of both the Saxon church and a later, medieval, one. The medieval church was demolished in the 1770s.

REFRESHMENTS:

The Air Hostess, Burnside Grove, Tollerton.

Walk 33   SUTTON-ON-TRENT   4m (6km)

Maps: OS Sheets Landranger 121; Pathfinder 781.
A short, but picturesque, walk along the River Trent.
Start: At 800657, the Lord Nelson Inn, Sutton-on-Trent.

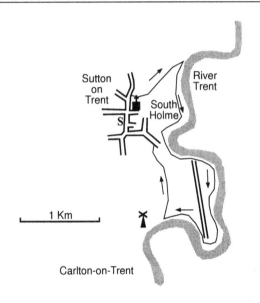

Parking is possible, with consideration, along Main Street. Walk north along Main Street. Main Street becomes Church Street: continue along it, passing the Council for the Preservation of Rural England's sign for the Best Kept Village and All Saints' Church. At the road junction, walk down Ingram Lane and turn right at the first farm entrance.

Follow the footpath sign along the narrow lane between a concrete bank, on the left, which belongs to the farm, and a garden fence, on the right. Go over a stile into a grassy field and cross this to reach an embankment. Now follow the yellow arrows on the fence posts over the embankment and through several grassy fields linked by stiles, heading north-eastwards. Go over a stile on to a broad grassy plain and maintain direction to cross a wide bridge over a dyke. Now turn right and walk southwards along the top of the grass embankment beside the **River Trent**. The embankment offers excellent views as the river meanders its way through its flat and fertile valley.

Walk along the embankment, enjoying the views, until a junction of embankments is reached close to the disused windmill at Carlton-on-Trent. Turn right and walk northwards along the higher embankment, heading back towards Sutton-on-Trent. Dominating the horizon behind the village are the cooling towers of the power station at High Marnham.

At the end of the embankment, follow the signed footpath through Manor Farm to reach Main Street. Turn right and walk back to the start.

POINTS OF INTEREST:

River Trent – At various times of the year the abundant wildlife will keep walkers entertained. Herons are common, as are ducks and geese. The anglers will be pleased to inform the walker of the nature (and the size!) of their catch.

REFRESHMENTS:

The Lord Nelson Inn, Main Street, Sutton-on-Trent.

Walk 34   **HUNGER HILL** $4^1/_2$m (7km)

Maps: OS Landranger 129; Pathfinder 813.
Excellent views of East Midlands scenery.
Start: At 664467, St Mary's Church, Lowdham.

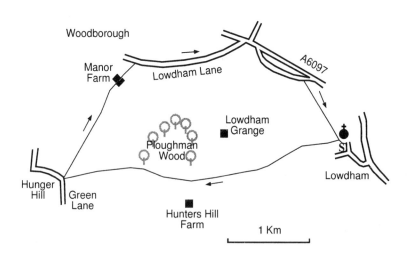

Parking is possible in Church Lane: please park considerately. To begin the walk, take the footpath along the side of the churchyard, leaving over a metal stile into the adjacent field. A path crosses the field westwards, but if ploughing is in progress it may be more pragmatic to walk around the edge of the field to reach the far corner. Here, yellow waymarker arrows direct you across a farm track and beside two more hedges to reach the tree-lined road leading to Lowdham Grange, formerly an institution for young offenders. Cross the road and a stile into a small meadow. Cross the meadow to reach a bridge over a ditch.

Cross the bridge, turn right and follow a green lane (bridleway) uphill. Lowdham Grange is to the right, concealed by the hedgerow. Briefly the route joins a farm track linking Hunters Hill Farm with Lowdham Grange. After 100 yards this track goes right: continue ahead (westwards) along the bridleway. When the bridleway ends, continue along a footpath, crossing the field ahead to reach a hedge. The views are extensive here, looking back over Lowdham and Lambley. At the hedge the path crosses another path going at right angles. A short cut is possible by going right, but for the best views you should maintain direction to reach a road (Green Lane). The views from here are excellent, looking over Lambley to Arnold and Gedling.

Now retrace your steps for 25 yards to reach an obvious gap in the hedge. Turn left here, following a well-defined path north-eastwards and descending towards Woodborough. From this path you will be treated to excellent views over Woodborough to Epperstone and beyond. The path maintains a straight line, following the hedgerows as it approaches Woodborough, and passing a Caravan Club site at Manor Farm before reaching Lowdham Lane. The route turns right here, but refreshments are available at the Nags Head Inn, 150 yards to the left.

Walk along Lowdham Lane, using the pavement to ensure that you are not at risk from passing cars or tractors. Follow the lane to its junction with the A6097, by Timmermans Nursery. Turn right and, with care, walk along the main road's wide grass verge for 75 yards, passing Knowles Garage, and then turning right along Old Epperstone Road. Follow the old road past the Springfield Inn. After following the road for about 800 yards, you will reach, on the right, the green-painted railings guarding a pumping station for the Severn-Trent Water Company. Here, turn right and walk for 50 yards to reach a barn. A hedge now leads off to the left over a hill: follow the path beside the hedge. Before long the spire of **St Mary's Church, Lowdham** will come into view directly ahead. Descend the path, heading towards the church and looking out for an unusual house to the left. The house, looking like a cross between a Wedgwood piece and a wedding cake, dominates the town of Lowdham. Continue along the path to return to the church.

POINTS OF INTEREST:
St Mary's Church, Lowdham – The church was founded in 1170 and has a Norman font and tower. Inside there is a stone effigy of Sir John de Lowdham.

REFRESHMENTS:
The Nags Head, Lowdham Lane, Woodborough.
The Springfield Inn, Old Epperstone Road, Lowdham.

Walk 35　　　**OWDAY WOOD**　　　4$\frac{1}{2}$m (7km)

Maps: OS Sheets Landranger 120; Pathfinder 744.

A walk across typical North Midlands farmland.

Start: At 588839, Carlton in Lindrick Church.

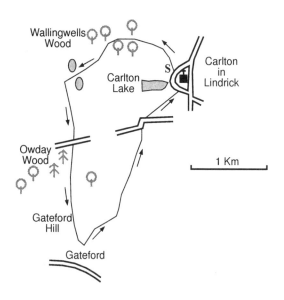

Cars can be parked in the large lay-by outside the church. Cross the road, go through the gap in the stone wall opposite and head north-north-west across a patch of ground used by fishermen as a car park. Go through a gate into a grassy field and follow a path across a raised embankment (which appears as an unfenced road on the map). To your left there is a small housing estate. Go through a gate into a small wood with a stone wall on the left. Beyond the wood the path goes along the side of an arable field, with a hedge on your left. Continue along the path into Wallingwells Wood. Follow the well-used track as it curves through the wood. This wood is much explored by local children so try to avoid the many side tracks they have created.

　　Follow the wide path that leaves the wood, crossing arable fields towards the twin lakes at Wallingwells. The lakes, which are initially out of sight, are managed by Wallingwells Angling Club. Go between the two lakes and continue along the path for 100 yards to reach a cross-tracks. Turn left (southwards) and follow this new bridleway, crossing a wooden bridge over a river and entering a small patch of woodland. The track curves gently left, and leaves the wood between a pair of stone gateposts to reach a corner of a farm track leading down to Wallingwells. Turn right and follow the track to meet a country lane at Owday Wood.

Cross the lane and go along the bridleway opposite. The bridleway goes along the edge of the wood, which is on your right: on your left is a hedge, with fields beyond it. Follow the path through a narrow spur of the wood to reach an arable field. Continue southwards along the edge of several fields, walking with a hedge on your right. The path becomes Owday Lane as it approaches Gateford on the outskirts of Worksop, and the lane becomes metalled as you pass the entrance to Gateford Hill.

Follow the lane into a new housing estate not marked on the OS map. However, the right of way still exists and can be followed without much difficulty. At a roundabout, go left along a prepared track, beside Ashes Park Avenue. Continue along the prepared track as it passes through a hedge on the left and then becomes a footpath crossing fields towards a small patch of woodland.

Go over a stone plinth in a hedge and continue along the path into the wood. On leaving the wood, a yellow footpath sign directs you across an arable field, pointing towards a tree in the middle. Behind the tree you can see the tower of Carlton Church: continue to reach a farm track at a sharp corner. Bear left to follow the track north-eastwards. There are good views of the local North Midland farm scenery on either side of the track. The track passes through a small wooded area to reach a road at a bend. Go straight ahead (northwards) along the road to reach Owday Lodge (at the next bend).

Now take the footpath just to the right of the Lodge. Follow this well-used footpath across two fields to reach the village of Carlton. A little alley now passes between stone cottages to reach the little river by Carlton Mill. Cross the footbridge over the river and walk back to the **Church of St John the Evangelist**.

POINTS OF INTEREST:

Church of St John the Evangelist – There has been a church on this spot for over 1,000 years. The church is mentioned in the Doomsday Book and Saxon work can still be seen in the tower. The west doorway is Norman, but the top storey and the buttresses reaching to the battlements are 15th-century.

REFRESHMENTS:

The Sherwood Range, Carlton in Lindrick.
The Bluebell Inn, Carlton in Lindrick.

Walk 36   HARLOW WOOD $4^{1}/_{2}$m (7km)

Maps: OS Sheets Landranger 120; Pathfinder 795.

A walk through a fine remnant section of Sherwood Forest.

Start: At 541558, the Forestry Commission car park, Thieves Wood.

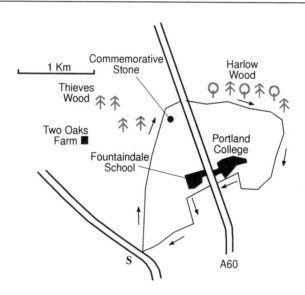

Leave the car park northwards, by a rustic barrier, to reach a sign offering a choice of waymarked walks. Go left along a broad lane following blue and white painted wooden posts. This lane is called the **King's Way**. Follow the track to the corner boundary of Two Oaks Farm. The white sign posts go off along a trail to the right, but our route continues to follow the blue-topped wooden posts northwards through the wood. Follow the track for 250 yards to reach a junction of tracks.

    Turn left, again following the blue-topped posts, for 250 yards, then turn right (now heading north-north-eastwards) and follow the track to reach a clearing, by some private houses, at the end of Thieves Wood Lane. Go eastwards along the lane, heading towards the A60.

Cross the A60 Mansfield to Nottingham Road, with great care as this road can be very busy, to reach the corner of Harlow Wood. Go past the log barrier and follow a forest track into the wood. The track bends right and then left as it goes deeper into this quiet section of woodland, passing behind the former Orthopaedic Hospital and Portland College. At a crossing of forest tracks, go straight over, heading south-eastwards. Soon you will come to a path on the left marked by green posts with white tops. This is the Friar Tuck Trail: turn left and follow the white-topped posts to reach a T-junction. Turn right and follow the white-topped posts to the Portland Training College for the Disabled where there is a cafe. Just before entering the college complex, the route turns left along a track to reach the A60.

Cross the road, again with great care, and walk along the path immediately opposite, passing a large rock positioned to stop vehicles entering Thieves Wood. Follow the path, now guided by signs for the Robin Hood Way, along the boundary of Fountaindale School. The path broadens out into a track, after parting company with the school's boundary fence: continue along the track to reach a complex junction of three tracks with a crossing path.

Here, a short diversion to the north-west – passing a picnic site – reaches a **Commemorative Stone**. The route heads south, and then south-east, along the track marked by blue and white posts of the King's Way. Turn left to continue following the blue and white posts to reach the boundary of the wood and Campfield Farm. Turn right and walk along the boundary track for about 450 yards, then, when the track goes right back into the woods, turn with it to return to the car park.

POINTS OF INTEREST:

The King's Way – This once was the main route joining the castles of Nottingham, Tickhill and Bolsover. It also became the main thoroughfare between Nottingham and Mansfield.

Commemorative Stone – This stone marks the spot the only Egyptian Nightjar known to have visited Britain was shot, on 3 June 1883. The bird was preserved and is now in Mansfield Museum.

REFRESHMENTS:

There is a cafe at the Portland Training College for the Disabled and, usually, a mobile café is parked in the starting car park. The nearest alternatives are in Ravenhead, a little way to the south-east.

Walk 37   **GOTHAM HILL**   5m (8km)

Maps: OS Sheets Landranger 129; Pathfinder 853 and 833.

A walk with an excellent viewpoint over south Nottinghamshire.

Start: At 537301, the Butter Cross in Gotham.

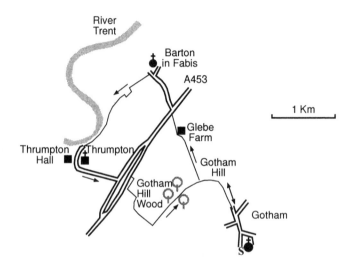

From the Butter Cross, outside the church, walk northwards, following the road out of the village. When the road makes a sharp right-hand bend by the British Legion Hall, continue straight ahead along a bridleway. The bridleway becomes a path winding its way through woods to the top of **Gotham Hill**.

From the top of the hill the walker is treated to magnificent views of south Nottinghamshire, and over the River Soar into North Leicestershire. Now cross the flat-topped hill to be greeted with views over the River Trent to Nottingham and east Derbyshire.

The route now follows a path which descends Gotham Hill, heading north-westwards to reach Glebe Farm. Follow the farm track to reach the A453. This is a very busy road as it is the main link between the M1 motorway and Nottingham, so please cross it with great care. Thankfully, at this point the walker has good views of the oncoming traffic in both directions. Follow the lane opposite into the small village of Barton in Fabis.

Turn left into Rectory Place, passing a farm entrance about 50 yards along the road. Turn left again to follow the clearly marked footpath for Thrumpton. Go over the stile and across the field beyond. In the distance you can see the cooling towers of the Ratcliffe on Soar Power Station. Follow the path over a flood embankment and across several fields, passing a pond to reach a farm track and another embankment beside the River Trent. This section of the route follows the Trent Valley Way. On the River Trent you will see both pleasure craft and wildlife, the latter including the Great Crested Grebe. Continue along the track into the village of Thrumpton, passing the gatehouse to Thrumpton Hall.

Take the lane out of Thrumpton, following it back towards the A453 to reach a T-junction. Turn left towards Barton, then, after 100 yards, turn right along a farm track, following the track across a bridge over the A453. Once over the main road, turn right for 150 yards, then turn left along a bridleway, following it through Gotham Hill Wood to return to the top of Gotham Hill.

Now reverse the outward journey to return to the village of Gotham.

POINTS OF INTEREST:

Gotham Hill – The hill offers the best views of south Nottinghamshire and north Leicestershire. From the top the view eastwards is across villages into the Vale of Belvoir, and southwards over the River Soar into north Leicestershire. To the north are the River Trent, with the city of Nottingham beyond, while to the west are the M1 motorway and, beyond, east Derbyshire.

REFRESHMENTS:
The Sun Inn, Gotham.
There are no pubs or shops in either Barton in Fabis or Thrumpton.

Walk 38   **WHATTON**   5m (8km)

Maps: OS Landranger 129; Pathfinder 813 and 834.

A walk through history.

Start: At 746393, Conery Lane, Whatton Green.

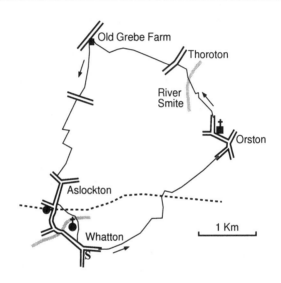

Parking is possible on Conery Lane, by the Green, but please park considerately. Walk eastwards down Orston Lane to the left of the Griffins Head Inn. After 50 yards the tarmac ceases, the lane becoming a farm track that crosses the River Whipling. Continue along the track for a mile to where it ends at the edge of a field. Here, the OS maps show a path crossing the field towards the railway line, but keeping to the edge of the field seems to be the custom. Once across the field the path becomes obvious: follow it through a hedge and northwards to the reach the railway line, the main rail link between Nottingham and Grantham. Just before going through a tunnel beneath the railway look out for a small pond that is well worth a few minutes of quiet observation.

You go under the railway at Bridge 23. Once on the other side, turn right and follow the railway for 100 yards to where the path goes into a coppice. Here you may either go straight through, following a track, or take a small diversion to the right to

74

reach a 'secret' pond, beside the railway line but hidden from view by hawthorns. This pond is a haven for wildlife. The diversion rejoins the track (Moor Lane) and follows it north-eastwards to the small village of Orston, coming out on the green by the village hall. Turn left along Mill Road, and left again into Loughbon, signed for Scarrington and Car Colston. Loughbon becomes The Green: continue along it, passing the church, and then turn right along High Street.

Walk northwards along High Street for 150 yards to where it becomes a dead end for cars, but offers a choice of two footpaths. Take the path on the left, signed for Thornton. Follow this well-used and equally well-marked footpath through several fields and hedges, crossing the River Smite and continuing into the village of Thornton. On reaching the village road, turn left for 50 yards, then turn right along a bridleway. Follow the bridleway north-westwards, crossing several fields to reach Old Grebe Farm and the Hawksworth/Scarrington road. Turn sharp left, southwards, following a path across yet more fields, heading towards Aslockton. Cross Longmoor Lane and maintain direction towards Aslockton. In the distance you will see the spire of Whatton Church.

The path reaches Mill Lane, on the outskirts of **Aslockton**: turn left towards the village, and, after 10 yards, turn right along Chapel Lane. Follow the lane to its end, then turn left along a jitty, following it to reach the main road in Aslockton opposite the Vicarage. Turn right and walk past St Thomas' Church and Cranmer's Cottage. Now, opposite Abbey Lane, take the footpath on the left. Cross the railway line, with great care, and continue along the footpath, crossing a meadow on a raised bank. Just before reaching the church in Whatton the path crosses the River Smite. Kingfishers can often be seen along this river. Continue to reach the **Church of St John of Beverley**. Here a choice of roads presents itself to the walker: either will do as they both lead to the Green and the start of the walk.

POINTS OF INTEREST:
Aslockton – The village is where Archbishop Thomas Cranmer was born in 1489.
Church of St John of Beverley – The church was where the young Thomas Cranmer worshipped with his father, before going to Cambridge University.

REFRESHMENTS:
Griffins Head Inn, Whatton.
The Durham Ox, Orston.
Cranmer Arms Inn, Aslockton.
The Old Greyhound, Aslockton.

Walk 39   RADCLIFFE ON TRENT   5m (8km)

Maps: OS Landranger 129; Pathfinder 813 and 834.

A cliff top walk along the River Trent.

Start: At 647392, the car park in Radcliffe on Trent.

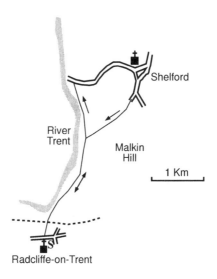

Leave the car park near the toilets and turn left along the main road. Walk past St Mary's Church, noticing the tower, which has an unusual tiled roof. Opposite the church is Wharf Lane: take this, passing a children's play area, and going underneath the Nottingham-Grantham railway line. Just under the railway you join the Trent Valley Way. Follow the path as it rises through woods above a residential caravan site. The path emerges from the woods into a linear park sandwiched between cliffs and the back gardens of some secluded houses, giving views of the River Trent and, beyond, towards Nottingham. Long-tailed tits are often seen on this section of the walk, and paths to the left offer the walker some interesting diversions down to the river. This route now stays at the top of the cliffs. When the linear park finishes, after about $^3/_4$ mile, continue through an avenue of hawthorns to reach the arable farmland that so typifies this area. Continue to walk above the river, with views to the right starting to appear. These views include the squat tower of **Shelford Church**. The path now gradually descends to the river, eventually following a raised bank, close to the water, with excellent views of the Ferry Boat Inn at Stoke Bardolph.

Continue along the path to reach Stoke Ferry Lane. Turn right and follow the lane into the village of Shelford. Walk past the church, leaving the village along West Street. When the road makes a sharp left turn, take the signed bridleway heading south-westwards towards Radcliffe on Trent. The track becomes a footpath: continue along this well-marked and well-used path along field edges to join the outward route by the avenue of hawthorns.

The route now reverses the outward journey. At the linear park, take time to visit the **Rockley Memorial Park**. Leave the park by following a path into Rockley Avenue and continue to the Shelford-Radcliffe road. Turn right and walk back into the village.

POINTS OF INTEREST:

Shelford Church – The name Shelford means the place of the shallow ford. The massive Perpendicular tower of the Church of St Peter and St Paul is a conspicuous feature in the Trent Valley. The village featured strongly during the Civil War when Royalist soldiers were smoked out of the church tower by Parliamentary troops.

Rockley Memorial Park – These gardens, and the adjoining woodlands, were presented to Radcliffe on Trent by Lisle Rockley in honoured memory of the men from Radcliffe who fell in the 1914-1918 War, but particularly as a memorial to Lt. William Lisle Rockley MC who was killed in action at Ypres on October 11, 1917.

REFRESHMENTS:
The Chesterfield Inn, Shelford.

Walk 40   COSSALL AND STRELLEY   5m (8km)

Maps: OS Landranger 129; Pathfinder 812.

A walk with views of south Nottinghamshire and east Derbyshire.
Start: At 485422, Robinettes Lane, Cossall.

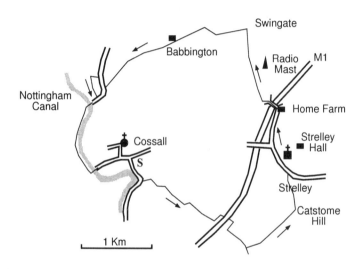

Walk southwards along the lane towards Trowel for 600 yards to reach a significant U bend where the lane crosses a tributary to the Nottingham Canal. Here, take the bridleway signed for Trowel and Balloon House, ascending a hill that gives views towards Strelley Hall, across the M1. Go through a couple of self-closing gates and continue to reach the motorway fence. Here, the path turns left for 200 yards before going under the road. On the other side, the path turns right for 200 yards to pick up the original line. About 400 yards beyond the motorway you will reach a crossroads of bridleways. Turn left to follow a section of the Robin Hood Way, heading north-east towards Catstone Hill. To the right you will see the city of Nottingham laid out as if it were a map. After $\frac{1}{2}$ mile the path goes through a gate to reach a confusion of paths, one to the right and three to the left. The first two left are tracks on to Catstone Hill. You want the third left, the one heading almost due north. Follow this track, which gives good views of Strelley Church, to reach a road. A right turn here will take you to Strelley's Broad Oak Inn, a diversion of about 400 yards.

The route turns left, passing All Saints' Church. Follow this quiet country lane to its end by Home Farm. Now take the signed bridleway for Swingate, soon crossing the M1. The bridge over the motorway gives good (if noisy) views, particularly to the south and west. Continue along the bridleway, passing a radio mast, one of two notable local features, the other being the tall, rectangular concrete water tower dominating the village of Swingate. The path enters the village beside the Queen Adelaide Inn: turn left, passing the water tower and some small cottages. At the end of the road take the bridleway for Babbington, descending with excellent views over the Erewash valley to east Derbyshire. A large signpost now directs you along a path into the hamlet of Babbington. Follow the narrow road down hill towards Awsworth for 500 yards, then, at a significant zig-zag, bear left along a signed path for Cossall, descending to reach the A6096. Cross, with care, and turn right for 50 yards to reach the driveway towards the small Decalkraft factory on the left. Take the path just to the left of the building, walk beside a paddock, cross a stile and turn left to walk along the division of two paddocks. Go over another stile into a thicket of hawthorns and follow a clearly defined path to regain the A6096 opposite Church Lane, Cossall. Turn right, with care, go under two bridges, and then take the path up to the towpath of the disused **Nottingham Canal**. Turn right to cross the A6096. The towpath is now a nature trail: follow it, with a glimpse of the dry ski slope at Cossall to reach a crossing farm track at Grid Reference 480419. Here, cross the canal and walk up Mill Lane to emerge directly opposite Robinettes Lane and the start of the walk.

POINTS OF INTEREST:

Nottingham Canal – The canal was opened in 1796. It is $14^3/_4$ miles long, linking the River Trent to the Comford and Erewash Canals at Langley Mill. William Jessop, the engineer, was one of the greatest of the canal builders. The canal was abandoned in 1937. In 1976 the Nottingham Canal Society was formed with the aim of restoring the canal for navigational purposes between Langley Mill and Trowel. However, open cast mining in the area has made this plan unrealistic. Lengths of the canal owned by Broxtowe Council are now managed for wildlife and as a public amenity. There is no longer any significant water in the canal, though the sections of standing water are interesting.

REFRESHMENTS:

The Chatterley Hotel, on the A6096 at Cossall.
The Broad Oak Inn, Strelley.
The Queen Adelaide, Swingate.

Walk 41   THISTLY COPPICE   5m (8km)

Maps: OS Landranger 129 and 120; Pathfinder 813 and 796.

A walk with exciting scenery.

Start: At 666471, on the wide grass verge beside the A6097, the Lowdham bypass.

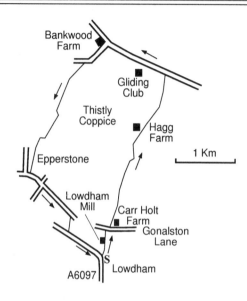

From the roadside parking, take the bridleway that heads northwards to Mill House. Turf for lawns is grown in the field on the left. On reaching the entrance to Lowdham Mill, take the footpath to the right of the mill, following it through an orchard. This path gives excellent views of the Mill House with its pond and mill race. Cross Dover Beck by way of a stile and bridge, and continue northwards, crossing a field to reach Gonalston Lane. Turn right along the lane for 100 yards, heading towards Carr Holt Farm, but turning left along a bridleway just before reaching it. Follow the bridleway northwards, with the farm on your right. The bridleway goes uphill through an 'alleyway' bounded by hawthorn hedges to emerge into a field near Hagg Farm. Cross a ditch by way a substantial wooden bridge: Hagg Cottage hides in the coppice on your right here. Now walk across the front yard of Hagg Farm, with fine views to the north, and east towards Thurgarton. Beyond the farm the path starts to descend as it approaches Souther Wood and Thurgarton Beck and on the hillside ahead the path that rises from the beck can clearly be seen. To the left is Thistly Coppice. The stone bridge across Thurgarton Beck was once a weir. Follow the bridleway uphill across fields. At the top of the hill, views of Thurgarton Park and beyond appear. Continue along the bridleway to reach an unmade road. Turn left and head towards Bankwood Farm, passing an airstrip belonging to the **Robin Hood Microlight Club**.

Continue to Bankwood Farm, passing a piggery and a poultry house on the left. Just before entering the farmyard, take a path on the left, by a willow tree. Follow the path around the side of the farm garden and pond, then descend towards a long and narrow coppice, crossing an equestrian course and then a rickety stile into the coppice. Follow the path uphill through the coppice to reach a ruined stone barn. At the barn the path goes left beside a hedgerow: continue along it to reach another coppice. Turn right and follow the edge of this coppice for about 250 yards. Yellow waymarkers now show you clearly the way through the coppice. Cross a ditch by way of a wooden footbridge and continue with a hedgerow on your left. This is the highest part of the walk, the view extending north-east as far as Newark. Footpath signs clearly show the way across the plateau, and soon the spire of Epperstone Church becomes visible. Follow the path downhill towards Epperstone, avoiding early opportunities to go into the village to reach the car park and beer garden of the Cross Keys Inn.

Continue to Main Street, Epperstone and turn left. Main Street becomes Gonalston Lane as you pass the turning, on the right, for the A6097. Go past the new, and angular, Epperstone Village Hall, also on the right, continuing along Gonalston Lane, or along the wide bridleway that runs beside it, for 800 yards. Now turn right through a kissing gate and follow a signed footpath across a meadow to reach the Paper Mill. Go through the yard, crossing Dover Beck again, and up the drive to the A6097. Turn left. The A6097 has a wide verge along which you can comfortably walk, but do take care as you follow the road back to the start of the walk.

POINTS OF INTEREST:

Robin Hood Microlight Club – In good weather the club fly their small craft from this airstrip. Walkers should enjoy the scene of the small craft taking off and landing and the intrepid can even buy a ticket for an aerial view of Nottinghamshire. The views from around here are some of the best in Nottinghamshire.

REFRESHMENTS:

The Cross Keys Inn, Epperstone.

Walk 42   **SOUTHWELL AND MORTON**   5m (8km)

Maps: OS Landranger 120; Pathfinder 796.

A fine walk offering excellent views of Southwell Minster.

Start: At 702538, the car park in Church Lane, Southwell, opposite the Minster.

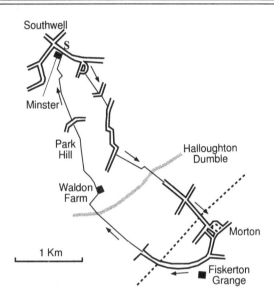

Turn left out of the car park and walk, with care, down Church Lane (the A612) towards Newark. Opposite the Hearty Goodfellow Inn, turn right into Farthingate. Now turn left into Farthingate Close and then take the footpath between Nos. 17 and 19. Follow the path into a paddock and cross a stile on the right into a field. Follow the path uphill across the field and into a wood. Look behind, when entering the wood, for a fine view of **Southwell Minster**.

Follow the yellow arrow waymarkers through the wood and into another paddock. Cross the paddock to reach a lane by Smithfield Cottage. Cross the lane and follow a footpath into some allotments for 5 yards, then go right, through a thicket, into a field. Cross the field to reach a track and turn right along it. Follow the track for about 700 yards, with good views to the left across the Trent Valley, to reach a bridleway sign pointing left through a gap in the hedge. Follow the bridleway as it zig-zags between fields. Cross a river (Halloughton Dumble) and continue along a track to reach a lane leading to Morton. Go straight ahead, along the lane, crossing the Nottingham to Newark railway, with care, at a level crossing with an old fashioned signal box (Fiskerton Junction). Continue along the lane into Morton.

Turn right by the Half Moon Inn and turn right again at the next junction. Follow the track to cross the railway line again (and, again, with care), continuing along it as it goes gently uphill and becomes a bridleway. Follow the bridleway as it goes over a slight hill and then descends to reach Halloughton Dumble again. Go left for 100 yards, then cross the river by way of a new gate and bridge. Now follow the bridleway uphill for 200 yards to reach a crossing lane. Turn right towards Waldon Farm, walking along the edge of Orwins Field. The path goes around the left side of the farm (heading west, then north) then crosses a field to reach a stile. Go over into a meadow. Continue along a well-marked path across several grassy fields, heading north-north-westwards and passing a small pond with observation platforms to reach a road.

Cross this minor road: you can now see the Minster nestling in the valley. Follow the path downhill towards the Minster, passing school playing fields and the Southwell City Football Club ground. Now walk through the grounds of the Minster to return to the car park.

POINTS OF INTEREST:
Southwell Minster – As the 'Mother Church' of Nottinghamshire, the Minster is the centre for many religious festivals. The two distinctive spires are known as the Pepper Pots. The Minster School is equally famous for its choristers.

REFRESHMENTS:
The Full Moon Inn, Morton.
The Hearty Goodfellow Inn, Southwell.
Southwell also offers many other places of refreshment.

Walk 43   **GOLDEN HILL**   5m (8km)

Maps: OS Sheets Landranger 120; Pathfinder 780.

A walk with historical interest and good views.

Start: At 724670, the Laxton Information Centre car park.

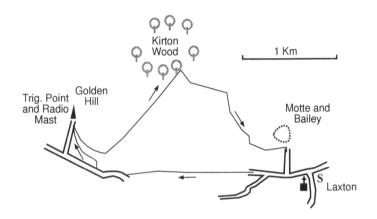

Leave the car park, beside the Dovecote Inn and the Information Centre, and cross the village green, walking towards the 12th-century Church of St Michael. Continue westwards along the main street and, at a Y-junction, maintain direction along the lane to the right. The lane becomes a track and then a green lane. Green lanes used to be the thoroughfares between field systems: they were also called Hollow Lanes because the passage of carts would wear the clay soil into grooves that lay below the surrounding fields.

You emerge from the green lane into open fields: maintain direction (westwards) with the radio mast on Golden Hill now clearly seen. After about 1,000 yards, the path goes right, then heads towards a white house to reach a road. Turn right (westwards) along the road for about 300 yards, passing the Beth Salom community, to reach a footpath sign on the right pointing to the Golden Hill radio mast.

Take this footpath, passing a small coppice and heading towards the radio mast. When the path meets a track coming up from the road, turn right and follow the fence that guards the mast, bearing left around the fence to reach the trig. point. The views to the west from here are excellent, with Sherwood Forest beyond the town of Ollerton and, beyond that, the Derbyshire Hills. To the north-west is Clumber Park and Worksop, while to the south-west is Wellow Park.

Now retrace your steps to the track and turn left to follow the bridleway back to the small coppice. Step through a hedge and cross a wooden bridge over a ditch. The path now crosses a field and a stile, then heads north-eastwards across arable fields, going downhill towards Kirton Wood. There are good views over the surrounding countryside and ahead to Egmanton on this section of the walk. Follow the northern edge of Kirton Wood to a crossing of footpaths signalled by a wooden bridge on the left.

Turn right and walk uphill beside a hedge. After 150 yards, cross a stile into an arable field and go diagonally across it. The other side of the field is out of sight, over a rise in the ground. Leave the field through a gate and walk along a track towards the village of Laxton. By a notice board, giving information about the unique system of farming in this village, go left over a stile and cross the small field beyond. Go over a stile on the left and walk along Hall Lane into Laxton Castle. Now take a track on the right, following it to reach the village of **Laxton** near the church. Turn left to return to the car park.

POINTS OF INTEREST:

Laxton – This is England's last open fields' village. Under the open field system, land use needs to be carefully regulated. At Laxton simple three course arable rotation is followed. In any year, one field is under winter wheat, the second has a spring crop such as barley, and the third is left fallow. The fallow field is used for grazing so that the sheep and cattle are providing manure. By 1967 the number of sheep and cattle had declined so the rules were changed to allow a forage crop to be grown and cut. There are no animals in the open fields today.

REFRESHMENTS:
The Dovecote Inn, Laxton.

Walk 44   EGMANTON WOOD   5m (8km)

Maps: OS Sheets Landranger 120; Pathfinder 780.

A walk of historic interest with good views.

Start: At 724670, the Laxton Information Centre car park.

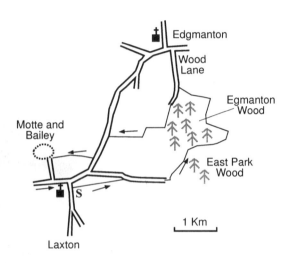

Turn right out of the car park and walk a few yards to reach the Pinfold. Inside is a notice explaining the features of Laxton. Between the Pinfold and a private house, there is a footpath going eastwards: take this, crossing a stile into a paddock. Cross a second stile into a grassy field, then go over a third stile, on the right, into an arable field. Turn left to continue walking eastwards, passing the local football ground and then following a path between fields. The path squeezes between two hedges as it nears a farm track. Turn right and walk along this track until it emerges into a field. From the track there are good views over the surrounding countryside.

Walk along the side of the field for 25 yards to reach a metal gate on the left. Go through the gate and head northwards across the field beyond, aiming towards a solitary oak tree. From it, head towards a second oak and then continue towards the edge of Egmanton Wood. Turn right and walk eastwards along the edge of the wood, passing through two hedges, then going over a stile by a gate and across a wooded bridge. Go through a second gate, this time without the help of a stile, and continue for a further 100 yards to reach a gap in the hedge on the left.

Go through this gap and continue along the edge of the wood for 200 yards, this time heading north-eastwards. Continue to follow the edge of the wood as it bends back north-westwards, then north-eastwards again and then, finally, heads due west. The path now reaches a track (Wood Lane): turn right along the track, following it, into the village of **Egmanton**. After visiting either the church or the village inn (or both), return to Wood Lane and reverse the route back to Egmanton Wood.

Now follow the west edge of the wood by continuing along the track, avoiding a branch going left into the wood. When the edge of the wood goes sharply left (eastwards), turn right (westwards) and walk along the boundary between two fields. Turn left at the hedge crossing the line of path and walk along the side of the field, with the hedge on your right. At a gap in the hedge you will join a track: follow this to the right to reach a double gate. Go through on to the Egmanton/Laxton road.

Turn left and walk along the road towards Laxton for 300 yards. The unique tower of Laxton Church can be seen clearly from here. At a bend in the road, turn right, go through a gate and walk westwards along the side of a field, keeping a hedge on your left. Step over a horse jump into a grassy paddock, and continue to reach the village cricket pitch. Continue westwards past the cricket pitch to reach a gate. Go through to reach a lane and a notice board explaining the history of **Laxton Castle**.

Turn left (southwards) and walk down the lane into Laxton, reaching the village opposite the church. Turn left to return to the car park at the Information Centre.

POINTS OF INTEREST:

Egmanton – The church in Egmanton has a shrine to Our Lady of Egmanton. Pilgrims come from all over Britain to visit the shrine which commemorates a vision of the Blessed Virgin in Ladywood. Parts of the church date back to medieval times.

Laxton Castle – The mounds are the finest example in Nottinghamshire of a motte and bailey fortification. The castle dates from the 11th century and was frequented by royalty including Henry 11 and Edward 1.

REFRESHMENTS:
The Old Plough, Egmanton.
The Dovecote Inn, Laxton.

Maps: OS Sheets Landranger 120; Pathfinder 796 and 780.
Magnificent views with a touch of history.
Start: At 651603, the Southwell Trail car park and picnic site.

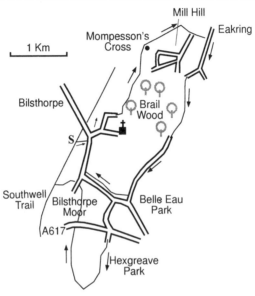

From the car park in Bilsthorpe, walk along 'Forest Link' through the housing estate to reach the Eakring to Kirklington road by a roundabout with a petrol station. Cross the road and walk along Brail Wood Road. After 200 yards, turn left along a footpath, following it northwards, and then eastwards to reach Eakring Brail Wood. Turn left (northwards) to follow a path along the western edge of the woods. Continue along the edge of the wood until it heads off eastwards (left), then head north-east across several fields, aiming to the left of a line of silver birch trees. At the trees, cross a small ditch and walk along a track, heading north-north-eastwards, that is not marked on the OS Landranger map. Follow this track to reach a road. Turn right along the road for 100 yards, to reach a sharp left corner before a steep hill. Here, turn right along a footpath, going uphill across an arable field to rejoin the road on the outskirts of Eakring. Those wanting refreshments can now walk the few yards into the village. The route continues by turning right along a path, heading south across a field to reach **Mompesson's Cross**. From the cross, turn left (eastwards) along a lane to reach a farm track. Cross the track and follow a footpath to Back Lane, Eakring. Cross the road into Side Road and walk down to Kirklington Road. Turn right (southwards) and walk along Kirklington Road for 400 yards. Now, when Kirklington Road bends left, bear right along Brail Lane. This unmade road becomes a bridleway: after 250 yards, turn left to follow a footpath southwards. Brail Wood can be seen on the right horizon from here. At a junction of paths, turn right. Follow the path past Brail Wood, keeping to the edge of the fields. As the path crosses the crest of a hill, and then goes through a hedge, you will be treated to splendid views over Kirklington. Continue along the path, crossing fields to reach a track near the Fox Holes Kennels and Cattery. Follow the track to Belle Eau Park, a small industrial estate. Continue to a road and turn right. Walk along the road for 250 yards to reach a lane on the left.

At this point the shorter walk continues along the road, heading north-westwards into Bilsthorpe and walking through the village to return to the start.

The longer walk turns left, following the lane to the main A617. Cross the road, with care, and turn left and then right into Hexgreave Park. Walk southwards along a beautiful avenue of beech trees to reach, as you emerge from the park, a footpath sign pointing right, diagonally across a field. Follow this path to reach a lane. Turn right and then immediately right again to follow a footpath across fields to reach the A617 again. Cross, again with care, and follow the path opposite, crossing several fields on Bilsthorpe Moor to reach the corner of a small wood on the outskirts of Bilsthorpe. Turn left to follow the edge of the wood to a road. Turn right along the road for 50 yards, then turn left along a path which follows the edges of fields to reach a bridge. Go under the bridge, then climb the embankment to reach the Southwell Trail. Turn right (northwards) and follow the Trail back to the start.

POINTS OF INTEREST:

Mompesson's Cross – William Mompesson worked in Eyam in 1665-66 during the Great Plague. Three years later he was appointed to the rectorship of Eakring, where the villagers were so afraid that he might still carry the disease that they made him live for a time in a hut in Rufford Park. The cross marks the spot where Mompesson preached during his exile.

REFRESHMENTS:

The Copper Beech, Bilsthorpe.
The Savile Arms, Eakring.

Walk 47   **LAMBLEY DUMBLE**   5m (8km)

Maps: OS Sheets Landranger 129; Pathfinder 813.

Typical Nottinghamshire scenery with excellent views.

Start: At 631454, Lambley Church.

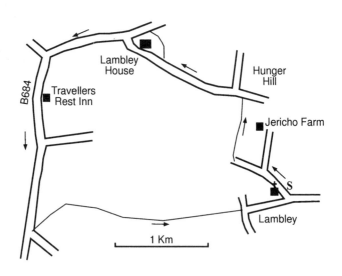

From the **church**, in Church Street, Lambley, walk out of the village, heading towards Woodborough. Go past the Woodcock Inn and then take the 'Dumbles': a public footpath sign shows the way. After 400 yards, at the end of the track, go right, over a stile, and follow the footpath beyond. The path then crosses grassy fields to reach Hunger Hill, passing Jericho Farm on the way. The path then crosses a grassy field through a line of trees. Go over another stile and cross several more grassy fields to reach Linwood Lane close to where it turns sharply right.

    Turn left, but do not follow the road: instead, follow the unmade track towards Lambley House. Follow the track for about 900 yards then, at the boundary of Lambley House follow the signposts which direct you to the right along a bridleway bounded by hedges on each side. Follow the bridleway to reach a road. Turn left (south-westwards) along the road. The road offers excellent views: to the right is Calverton and, behind, Woodborough, while to the left is Lambley.

Follow the lane to the B684 and turn left. Follow the main road, with care, passing the Mellish Rugby Football Club and the Travellers Rest Inn, before reaching Spring Lane, on the left. Turn along Spring Lane, and then immediately go left again along the signed footpath towards Lambley.

Follow the well-used footpath across fields, going over stiles and through hedges as you walk beside the Lambley Dumble towards the village of Lambley. The path emerges by the playing area for the primary school, opposite the Nags Head Inn: walk back along Main Street to reach **Lambley Spring** and the start of the walk.

POINTS OF INTEREST:

Lambley Church – The church was rebuilt by Lord Ralph Cromwell. Born in Lambley, Cromwell became the Lord Treasurer to Henry VI and presented Parliament with its first budget. The church is a fitting memorial and is one of the few remaining Perpendicular churches in Nottinghamshire.

Lambley Spring – The settlement of Lambley is thought to be of Roman origin, possibly a military outpost that guarded a by-road from the Foss Way and overlooked the Trent Ferry at *Marsidunum* (East Bridgford).

REFRESHMENTS:
The Travellers Rest, Arnold.
The Woodlark Inn, Lambley.
The Nags Head, Lambley.
The Robin Hood Inn, Lambley.

Walk 48 NORTH WHEATLEY TO CLARBOROUGH 5m (8km)
Maps: OS Sheets Landranger 120; Pathfinder 745.

A walk along green lanes, with excellent views across high North Midlands farmland.

Start: At 755858, Low Street, North Wheatley.

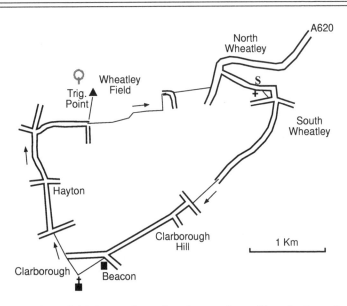

Car parking is available in Low Street, but please park considerately. From the Sun Inn walk along Low Street, **North Wheatley**, towards the smaller hamlet of South Wheatley. Just after passing the Methodist Chapel, by the footbridge, step left into a field and cross it to reach a sharp bend in a road in South Wheatley, by Corner Farm.

Now go southwards along Muspitts Lane, a bridleway. The bridleway veers southwest as it ascends Clarborough Hill: continue along it, with extensive views opening out over North Wheatley. There is also a good view of the West Burton Power Station.

The green lane now peters out, becoming a wide path: continue along the path to reach a junction of green lanes. Turn right for 50 yards, then turn left along a green lane that will take you to the top of **Clarborough Hill**. Continue to reach another junction of green lanes.

Take the footpath signed for Clarborough, keeping a hedge on your right as you follow the path steeply downhill towards the church. Near Clarborough Church, take the path going right, through a hedge. Follow the path across the bottom of a narrow field, then over a stile into a wild area which is good for blackberries in September. Continue along the well-defined path to reach a green lane. Cross the lane, going left, then right, and continue following the footpath signs across a grassy field. There is a warning notice about a bull in the field, so keep a look out. Go over a stile into an arable field and walk along its edge to reach the A620.

Cross, with care, and continue northwards along a green lane for a mile to reach a cross-tracks. Those wanting refreshments can turn left here to reach the Boat Inn at Hayton, a detour of about a mile there and back. The route turns right (eastwards), following a green lane as it ascends Wheatley Field. When the lane makes a sharp right turn, you can go left for a short detour to the summit trig. point, 68 metres (223 feet) above sea level. Despite the low altitude this is a fine spot, with excellent views into South Yorkshire, Derbyshire and Lincolnshire, where Lincoln Cathedral can be seen.

Back on the route, follow the signed footpath eastwards, towards North Wheatley, crossing fields linked by stiles: a left and right zig-zag, following hedges, is the only deviation from the straight line. The path approaches Wheatley Field Farm along the boundary between two fields: turn left at the farm hedgerow and walk beside the tall hedge of conifers for 200 yards to reach a farm track.

Turn right along the track, following it as it becomes a green lane heading eastwards. The lane emerges on to the A620 road opposite the Sun Inn.

POINTS OF INTEREST:
North Wheatley – A village full of character. Many of the streets retain their original names from the days when agriculture was a more labour intensive business.
Clarborough Hill – The hill offers fine views over four counties, Nottinghamshire, Derbyshire, South Yorkshire and Lincolnshire. On top is a beacon left over from the Queen's Jubilee celebrations and a more obtrusive tower clothed in microwave dishes.

REFRESHMENTS:
The Sun Inn, North Wheatley.
The Boat Inn, Hayton.

Walk 49   **DORKET HEAD**   5m (8km)

Maps: OS Sheets Landranger 129; Pathfinder 813 and 812.

A walk through beautiful East Midlands farmland with excellent views.

Start: At 631477, St Swithun's Church, Woodborough.

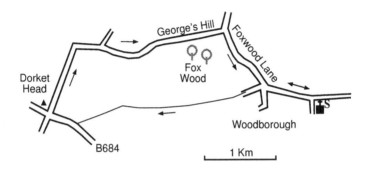

From the Parish Church of St Swithun, **Woodborough**, walk westwards along Main Street (along which Woodborough Beck also makes its way) for 1,100 yards to reach a road junction. Bear right along Foxwood Lane, then, after 50 yards, turn left along a signed bridleway (West Field Lane). After 300 yards this unmade road becomes a track across open fields.

Follow the bridleway through a valley, keeping a stream to your right. Occasionally the hedgerow is close on your right, at other times it is 50 yards or so further off. The track crosses arable fields and some fields used by the nursery Timermans for starting their roses, going through several gates or over stiles. Finally a footpath sign indicates a change of direction: bear left to follow a path uphill, away from the valley, walking with a hedge on your left.

At the top of the hill the path goes through a hedge to reach the B684. Turn right, with care, and follow the road 350 yards to reach a crossroads at the top of Dorket Head. There is a trig. point (at 146 metres – 479 feet) marking the top of the hill. From this point the walker has excellent 360° views over Nottinghamshire.

Now turn right, taking the country lane heading north towards Calverton. The views eastwards (to the right) across to Woodborough from this road are excellent. The road bends sharp right, and then, after another 400 yards, sharp left by a mock Tudor House. At this second bend, continue straight ahead (eastwards) along a bridleway – a green lane known as George's Hill. The bridleway keeps to the crest of a ridge as it approaches Fox Wood. The views on both sides are excellent: to the left is Calverton, while on the right Woodborough can be seen.

Follow the bridleway to Foxwood Lane. Turn right and walk along the lane, going downhill into the village of Woodborough. The outward route is rejoined close to Main Street, which is then followed back to the start.

POINTS OF INTEREST:

Woodborough – From the 16th century Woodborough was a centre for framework knitting, as witnessed by many of the cottage windows and old knitters' workshops still in existence. As recently as 1844 there were still 191 frames working in the village. Note the inscription under the gable of Hall Farm House, built by Philip Lacock in 1710.

REFRESHMENTS:
The Four Bells, Woodborough.

Walk 50   TITHBY   5m (8km)

Maps: OS Sheets Landranger 129; Pathfinder 834.

A walk through two charming villages.

Start: At 701391, by the side of the A52, south of Bingham.

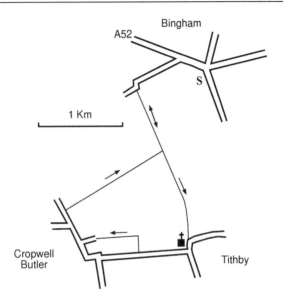

The walk starts on the southern side of the A52, the Bingham bypass, at its junction with Tithby Road, where limited parking is available. Walk westwards along a farm track. After 400 yards the track reaches a hedge and veers to the left: continue along the track for a further 550 yards, then turn left to follow the footpath on the left-hand side of a hedge. The path maintains a straight line course for about 1,100 yards, passing through two hedges going off to the left. Cross a farm track and continue following the hedgerow. The path zig-zags before crossing a ditch and then crosses another field to reach the hamlet of Tithby.

Walk through this charming hamlet, which consists of a couple of farms, **Holy Trinity Church** and some houses, to reach a road junction. Turn right, looking out for the old AA road sign on a white cottage, and walk along the road for 650 yards. Now turn right along a footpath, following it diagonally across a field to reach a stile. Go over and cross another field. Now go over two stiles to cross a ditch and turn left along a footpath, following it as it becomes a track and passes the Village Hall before reaching the main road in the village of Cropwell Butler.

Turn left along the road if you wish to visit the Plough Inn. The route turns right towards the charming, triangular village green. Take Hardigate Road out of the village, following it for 200 yards before turning right along a track leading north-eastwards. Follow this track for just under a mile to reach the path followed on the outward journey. Now turn left and reverse the outward route back to the start.

POINTS OF INTEREST:

Holy Trinity Church, Tithby – The church is famous for its 14th-century font and Priest's door. It also has Georgian furnishings and a double-decker pulpit. The brick tower has an unusual pyramidal top.

REFRESHMENTS:

The Plough Inn, Cropwell Butler.

Maps: OS Sheets Landranger 129; Pathfinder 834 and 854.
Magnificent views over the Vale of Belvoir.
Start: At 691295, Hickling Wharf.

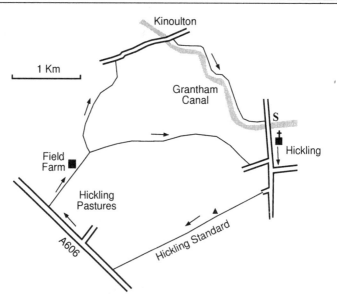

The walk starts opposite the Plough Inn: go southwards along the road, passing the
church, on the left, and the Post Office and stores, on the right. Turn right up an
unmade lane opposite Harles Acres. The road becomes a narrow bridleway: continue
along it, uphill, and, at the top, go left, over a stile, into a grassy field. Now go right,
following yellow waymarkers uphill, crossing stiles to reach the top of **Hickling
Standard**. Continue to follow the path signs, crossing stiles and fields to reach the
A606. Turn right and, with care, follow the broad verge through Hickling Pastures.
Walk past Bridegate Lane, continuing along the main road to reach a signed footpath
on the right, opposite Fox and Hounds Farm. Go over the stile and follow the path
through a small wooded area. Cross another stile and maintain direction across a field
to reach a pair of stiles. Beyond there is a choice of paths: take that on the left, following

yellow waymarkers over stiles and across fields to reach a strategically placed seat near Field Farm. Across the valley from here Hickling Standard forms the horizon, while down the valley is Hickling and, beyond, the Vale Of Belvoir. Go along the edge of an arable field by Field Farm to reach a junction where the path crosses a bridleway.

The shorter walk goes over the stile by a gate into a field. Now follow the yellow arrows across fields towards the village of Hickling, finally going through a gate to reach Bridegate Lane. Turn left and follow the lane into Hickling. At the end of Bridegate Lane, turn left to return to the start of the walk at Hickling Wharf.

The longer route turns left and follows the bridleway uphill. After 50 yards the bridleway goes through a gate in the hedge and continues north-westwards. After a further 70 yards, go through a dilapidated gate and cross a small ditch. Here you branch left (north-east), heading diagonally across an arable field. Cross a stile and take a diagonal line across the grassy field beyond. Go though a gate and cross another grassy field to reach a hedge on the corner. Now follow the hedge to reach a stile by Blacks Farm. Go over and walk along the path beyond, beside Blacks Farm, to reach Kinoulton Lane. Turn right and walk into the beautiful village of Kinoulton with its fine red-brick cottages. Go past the 'Old School House' and cross the **Grantham Canal**. Now turn right along the canal towpath which gives a pleasant walk for the $1^1/_4$ miles back to the start.

POINTS OF INTEREST:

Hickling Standard – From the trig. point (at 105 metres – 344 feet) at the summit there are excellent views over south Nottinghamshire and north Leicestershire.

Grantham Canal – Building of the canal started in 1793 and it was fully navigable in 1797. The canal was soon adopted as a focal point for local activities. Originally there were two wharves, one on the basin side, now called Wharf Yard, the other across the road. The latter is now the front lawn of Bridge View, formerly the Navigation Inn. The canal was an important trading link between Lincolnshire and Nottingham. Eventually the Nottingham to Grantham railway line killed the commercial use of the canal. Today it has been renovated and is an important area for wildlife and much frequented by anglers.

REFRESHMENTS:
The Plough Inn, Hickling.

Maps: OS Sheets Landranger 120; Pathfinder 763.
Superb walking through one of the famous Dukeries estates.
Start: At 646773, the Apleyhead Wood car park.

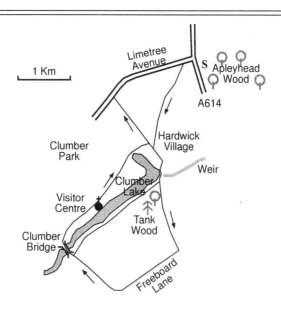

The Apleyhead Wood car park is opposite the Apleyhead Gate into **Clumber Park**.
From it, cross the A614, with care, walk through the arch of Apleyhead Gate and go
along the road beyond for 100 yards. Now take a signed footpath on the left, heading
south-westwards and following yellow waymarkers through the wood. Cross a farm
track and continue into an arable field. Go through a small clump of trees to reach a
track, and turn right, still following the yellow arrows. After 200 yards, follow the
yellow arrows across a field on the left to reach a house in a clump of trees. Follow
the path around the house and then across another field to reach Hardwick Wood. Go
through the wood and cross a stile by a gate on to a road. Turn left and walk into
unspoilt **Hardwick Village**. Walk through this charming village to reach a T-junction.

Turn right to reach Clumber Lake just north of the weir. There are public toilets near here. Cross the weir heading southwards. To the east of the weir the marshy ground beside the River Poulter is a Wildfowl Sanctuary. To the west of the weir is Clumber Lake which is also home to a variety of water birds.

From the southern side of the weir the shorter walk follows a well-trodden path along the bank of the lake to reach Clumber Bridge. This route offers plenty of opportunity for spotting the area's water birds.

The longer walk takes the alternative path southwards through Tank Wood and across heathland to reach Freeboard Lane. The National Trust has an unusual design of wooden kissing gate in their fences hereabouts. You will also pass a number of strange rustic structures indicating that the area is frequently used for equestrian events. Cross a stile on to Freeboard Lane and turn right to follow it for about a mile to reach a distinct path through the heathland on the right. Follow this path to reach Clumber Lake near Clumber Bridge.

The routes reunite at Clumber bridge. Cross the bridge and turn right into Lady Garden to visit **Clumber Grotto**. You can also visit the tea rooms. Go north out of the Tea Rooms complex and follow the path across a field to reach Ash Tree Hill Wood. Go over a stile into the woods and continue along a track. Follow the track to reach the top of Clumber Lake near Hardwick Village. Cross the metalled road and walk northwards beside the final tip of the lake. Note that this section of the lake is not marked on older OS maps. When you reach a road, turn right to follow it into Hardwick Wood. The road reaches a junction with the road leading into Hardwick Village: turn left and walk up to Limetree Avenue. Turn right and walk beneath the lime trees back to Apleyhead Gate and the start of the walk.

POINTS OF INTEREST:
Clumber Park – The park was originally created in the 18th century as a country seat for the Duke of Newcastle. It was acquired by the National Trust in 1946.
Hardwick Village – This unspoilt village lies deep in the bounds of Clumber Park. Both the post and telephone boxes are painted green.
Clumber Grotto – The building housed the water pump for the estate. Water was pumped from an artesian well into an underground reservoir.

REFRESHMENTS:
The Clumber Park Tea Rooms, on the route.

Walk 55   REMPSTONE   5m (8km)

Maps: OS Sheets Landranger 129; Pathfinder 853.
Through East Midlands farmland.
Start: At 575245, All Saints Church, Rempstone.

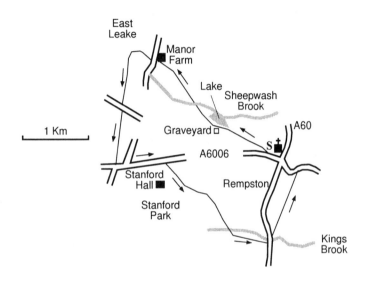

From the corner of the church car park, take the footpath across fields towards East Leake. On the horizon, just to the right of the line of walking, you will see the cooling towers of the power station at Ratcliffe on Soar. The path crosses five arable fields: at certain times these may be ploughed, but this is a popular route and so the path is unlikely to disappear for long. Go through a hawthorn hedge and over a stile into an overgrown graveyard, the site of **St Peter in the Rushes Church**. Keep to the northern edge of the graveyard. On the other side of the hedge is a private lake feed by the Sheepwash Brook. Follow the boundary fence to the pond to the right and continue along a path towards Manor Farm. Cross a wooden bridge through a hedgerow and follow yellow arrows for 15 yards before turning right to cross another wooden bridge into a grassy field. Turn left and follow a well-marked path to Manor Farm, a children's study farm with a collection of animals such as guinea fowl and pot-bellied pigs. At the farm the path has been redirected: go to the north of the farm, following the path to Mill Lane. Turn left and follow the lane to a road.

Cross the road and follow the footpath opposite across three grassy fields on the outskirts of East Leake. At the corner of the last field turn left and follow the hedgerow southwards across grassy fields. Cross a concrete bridge into another grassy field and go over a stile into a third field. Cross another stile on to a lane. Go left for about 10 yards, then turn right along a signed path by a gate and stile. Follow a path with a hedge on your right, then cross a stile and a wooden bridge to reach a farm lane. Go around the buildings on the right, then turn left into the field. Walk around the edge of the field, keeping the hedge on your right, to reach a stile and a bridge over a ditch beside an isolated tree. Cross into a grassy field and turn left to walk around the edge, with a hedge to the left, to reach a stile on to the A6006. Turn left along the broad grassy verge for 750 yards, passing the entrance to Stanford Hall, an International Training College for the Co-operative Movement. At the edge of the Hall's grounds, cross the road, with care, and turn right along a bridleway, following it beside the walled grounds of Stanford Hall. The bridleway reaches a gate where the wall turns right: head south-eastwards across the next field to reach Kings Brook. A notice by the brook warns horse riders that the bridleway will cease mid-stream: this is the boundary between Nottinghamshire and Leicestershire and you are about to (briefly) cross counties.

Go through a gate to reach Kings Brook. There is no bridge, but a large stone mid-stream helps you over. Turn left and walk along the brook's bank. Follow the path through a hedge and up a bank to reach the A60. Cross, with care, turn left and head northwards along the grassy verge for 10 yards to reach a bend in the road. You are now back in Nottinghamshire. Take the signed footpath on the right, following it up Sutcliffe Hill, keeping a hedge on your left. The hill offers excellent views over the surrounding Nottinghamshire and Leicestershire countryside. Descend the hill across park land into the village of Rempstone, arriving at the A6006 opposite the White Lion Inn. Turn left and walk along Main Street to reach the A60. Cross the A60 at the traffic lights and walk back to All Saints Church.

POINTS OF INTEREST:
St Peter in the Rushes Church – Only the gravestones remain to mark the site of this church. Much of its stone was used in the construction of All Saints Church, Rempstone.

REFRESHMENTS:
The White Lion Inn, Rempstone.

Walk 56   **RUDDINGTON COUNTRY PARK**   5m (8km)

Maps: OS Sheets Landranger 129; Pathfinder 833.

A fine walk mixing heritage and history.

Start: At 575321, the car park at the Rushcliffe Country Park, Ruddington.

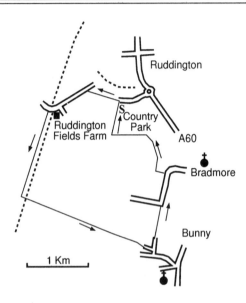

Leave the **Rushcliffe Country Park** car park through the gate at its western end and follow a gravel path running parallel to the **Great Central Railway Line**. As an embankment obscures the view the pedestrian bridge must be used to see the steam trains as they go in and out of the marshalling yard. Continue along the gravel path to reach the railway level crossing at Asher Lane. Turn left along Asher Lane, leaving the Country Park. Follow Asher Lane to Ruddington Fields Farm where footpath signs direct you to a bridge over another railway line. Once across, turn left and follow a well-marked footpath beside the railway. The path is relatively new and trees have been planted between it and the fields. When they become established these trees will shield the walker from the prevailing wind that comes across Ruddington Moor. To the right, across the moor, you can see Gotham Hill.

When the path reaches Fairham Brook, turn right, crossing a stile, the railway line and another stile into an arable field. Initially beside the brook, the path goes through a hedge and then heads south-westwards beside a hedge. The path widens to become a broad green swath between arable fields: continue along it, passing a track going off to the left. At the end of the green swath, turn left (north-eastwards) for 25 yards to reach a wooden bridge. Cross and walk towards an intimidating notice declaring 'Private Property - No Footpath'. Turn right and walk south-eastwards beside a ditch. The path becomes enclosed between hedges, and then becomes a farm lane leading into Bunny: turn right at a T-junction and then left at another T-junction to reach Moor Lane, Bunny.

After exploring the picturesque village of Bunny with its fine church, return along Moor Lane and turn right (northwards) along a farm lane, passing the lane by which you entered Bunny. The lane reduces to a footpath between fields as you continue north towards Bradmore, its church spire showing clearly just right of the line of walking. Follow the path to reach a farm lane. By the entrance to the lane you will see a rustic seat in memory of 'Syd, who walked this way every morning with Moss'.

Follow the lane into Bradmore, taking time to explore this charming village with its unique church before returning to the point of entry. Walk down Littlemoor Lane to reach a signed footpath which leaves the village westwards through a wooden kissing gate. Go down a field, walking beside a hedgerow and, at the end of the field, go right to follow the hedgerow northwards. The hedgerow is on your right. Go over a low stile from the field into another, continuing with the hedgerow now on the left to reach a concrete road going around the edge of Rushcliffe Country Park.

Cross the road and enter the park through an open gate to reach a gravel pathway. Turn left and follow the pathway around the park. A path on the right will now lead you across the park to reach a lake and the car park.

POINTS OF INTEREST:
Rushcliffe Country Park – The Park has been created on the site of a former MOD Ordnance Depot.
Great Central Railway Line – The railway is now run by enthusiasts. It is planned to connect it to both Nottingham and Loughborough.

REFRESHMENTS:
The White Horse Inn, Church Street, Ruddington.
The Rancliffe Arms, Bunny.

Walk 57   **CROMWELL LOCK**   5m (8km)

Maps: OS Sheets Landranger 121; Pathfinders 780 and 781.

A walk along the River Trent visiting a picturesque lock.

Start: At 799615, St Giles Church, Cromwell.

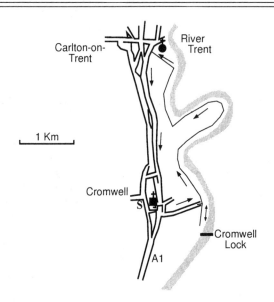

Parking is possible, with consideration, along Main Street. From the church, walk southwards along Main Street, passing the Doll Museum. Turn left opposite the telephone box and walk through a farmyard. Turn left, and then right to go over a bridge crossing the A1. Turn right, and then left to walk towards the River Trent. The 'Private Road' notice refers only to the use of cars along this lane.

Follow the lane through fields to reach the river (though the river is out of site behind a large earth bank). At a sharp bend, follow the lane to the right and walk to the picturesque **Cromwell Lock**. Return along the track to the sharp bend, then step through the hedge straight ahead and now head northwards along the riverbank of the Trent, walking along the top of the grassy embankment. Keep to the raised embankment as the river meanders its way through fertile farmland. Sand and gravel pits can be seen on both sides of the river: these provide a fine habitat for waterfowl. You will also see a variety of boats on the river, while anglers enjoy fishing from the banks.

Continue along the top of the embankment as it curves westwards and leaves the river, far enough to allow fields to develop on the river side. When you arrive at a dyke with a bridge, cross the bridge and walk along the side of the dyke to return to the river. Turn left and walk along the raised riverbank to reach a fence. The stile is missing, so climb over the fence and continue northwards through the grassy field beyond to reach a hedge. Walk around the hedge, then cross heathland, aiming directly for the spire of the church at Carlton-on-Trent. Cross a ditch over a farm bridge and go over a stile on to a lane. Turn left and walk along the lane to reach Church Street, Carlton-on-Trent, beside the Church of St Mary the Virgin.

Turn left along Church Street to reach Main Street. Go past the Old Forge and continue along Main Street, which becomes Great North Road. Continue along this quiet country lane (which runs beside the busy A1 trunk road) for about a mile to reach a bridge. Turn right over the bridge, crossing the A1 to return to Cromwell.

POINTS OF INTEREST:
Cromwell Lock – A stone in the trees by the lock marks the discovery, in 1884, of the remains of a Roman bridge in the river bed nearby. Near the lock is a memorial to 10 Sapper volunteers of the 131 Independent Parachute Squadron, Royal Engineers, who died at the weir whilst on an exercise on 28 September 1975.

REFRESHMENTS:
The Nags Head, Carlton-on-Trent.

Walk 58   **BINGHAM AND CAR COLSTON**   5$^1/_2$m (9km)

Maps: OS Sheets Landranger 129; Pathfinder 813 and 834(but only for the first few yards).

A walk across typical East Midlands farm land.

Start: At 705399, Bingham Market Square. Parking is possible either in the Market Square or in Station Road.

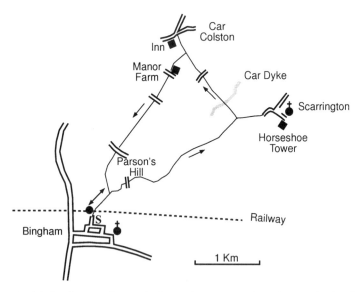

From the Market Square, close to the Butter Cross, go northwards along Station Road and cross the railway by way of the rather metallic footbridge to reach Butt Field. Cross the field, avoiding any sports that may be playing at the time, to reach the far (north-eastern) corner. There, leave the playing field, bearing right to go eastwards along the side of the field. Cross a track and continue along waymarked paths towards Scarrington. At certain seasons it is better to use the larger scale map, as the field boundaries are marked, making navigation easier.

When you reach a footpath junction, the route turns left towards Car Colston. To the right here, Scarrington Church can be seen. A short diversion into **Scarrington** is worthwhile: opposite the Church is the Old Forge, outside of which is a wonderful tower made of around 50,000 old horseshoes, topped by a crown looking like a Viking Helmet. However, it is worth noting that Scarrington does not have either an inn or a shop.

At the footpath junction, take the path towards Car Colston, heading north-westwards across Car Dyke. The path is well waymarked, and before long develops into a track. As you near Car Colston, the village church, with its squat tower, is clearly visible. Continue to reach the village green, just to the right of the Royal Oak Inn and the cricket pitch. Follow the southern edge of the green and cross a footbridge, that passes through a hedge and over a ditch, into a field normally occupied by sheep. Now follow the well-marked footpath through fields and hedges and over ditches to reach a path junction and a footbridge. Continue southwards over Parsons Hill to return to the Butt playing field. Now reverse the outward route back into **Bingham**.

POINTS OF INTEREST:
Scarrington – The present Smithy building dates from about 1840, though it is believed there has been a forge here for at least 300 years. The tower of horseshoes stands 17 feet (about 5 metres) high and has a circumference of 19 feet 6 inches (almost 6 metres) at its base. The horseshoes are interlocked, so no glue or cement has been needed to keep them from collapsing. The tower is estimated to weigh about 10 tons and is believed to be the largest stack of used horseshoes in the world. Nottinghamshire County Council bought the tower in 1973 to prevent it from going to America. Some remedial work was necessary in 1987/8. Lately, souvenir hunters and general disintegration have caused the tower to develop a Pisa-like lean.
Bingham – The Butter Cross in the Market Square was built, in 1860, in remembrance of John Hassan of Shelford. Inscribed on it is the delightful thought 'To be beloved is better than all bargains'.

REFRESHMENTS:
The Royal Oak, Car Colston.
There are a number of inns and a cafe in Bingham.

Walk 59   **BURTON JOYCE** $5^1/_2$m (9km)

Maps: OS Sheets Landranger 129; Pathfinder 813.

A walk offering excellent views of the Trent Valley.

Start: At 646431, the Stoke Bardolph Estate car park.

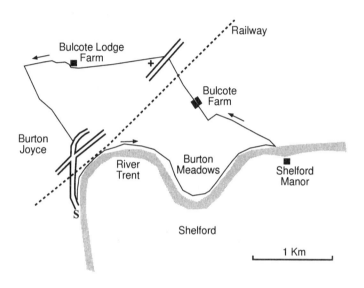

The car park lies on a bank of the **River Trent**, to the south of Burton Joyce. From it, turn left and walk along the banks of the river, heading towards Burton Joyce. Stay on the riverbank as the Trent skirts Burton Joyce – the village lying just to the north. On this section of the walk there are excellent views of the surrounding farmland, and the tower of Shelford Church stands out across the river. Now walk around Burton Meadows, from where you will get a glimpse of Gunthorpe Bridge and the old windmill at Kneeton.

At Grid Reference 671437 (Angler's Marker Post No. 52) turn left, leaving the river and walking towards the gravel pit lakes. Now follow a bridleway across fields towards Bulcote. The bridleway passes Bulcote Farm with its magnificent brick buildings surrounding a cobblestone courtyard. A large set of locked wrought iron gates prevents the walker from exploring the courtyard. The farm is now owned by

110

the Severn-Trent Water Company. Cross the railway line, with care, at the level crossing and continue for a further 50 yards to reach the main road in the village of **Bulcote**. Maintain direction along the road (heading north-eastwards), passing a telephone box before reaching Ivy Cottage and Ivy House, and the main A612, Nottingham to Southwell road, opposite Holy Trinity Church. Cross the road, with care, and follow the bridleway, signed for Lambley, beside the church.

The bridleway climbs above Burton Joyce, offering fine views of the River Trent and south Nottinghamshire. Follow the bridleway past Bulcote Lodge Farm, continuing to reach a T-junction at Grid Reference 639447. Here, turn left (south-eastwards) and follow a bridle road as it descends into Burton Joyce, passing quiet detached houses. The bridle road joins Lambley Road: continue to descend into Burton Joyce passing the ornate Burton Joyce United Reform Church. At the War Memorial, turn right along Nottingham Road. Cross the A612, with care, and go along Station Road opposite. Cross the railway at the level crossing by the station, also with care, and continue along the Stoke Bardolph road to reach the starting car park.

POINTS OF INTEREST:

River Trent – At all times of the year the abundant wildlife will keep walkers entertained. Herons are common as are ducks and geese, and anglers will be pleased to inform you about the nature (and the size) of their catch.

Bulcote – Ivy House was formerly the village pub, the Unicorn. Holy Trinity Church retains the 1662 liturgy.

REFRESHMENTS:

There are numerous opportunities in Burton Joyce.

Walk 60   **EAKRING AND MAPLEBECK**   5¹/₂m (9km)

Maps: OS Landranger 120; Pathfinder 780 and 796.

Excellent scenery and an enchanting wood.

Start: At 674619, beside the Eakring to Kirklington road.

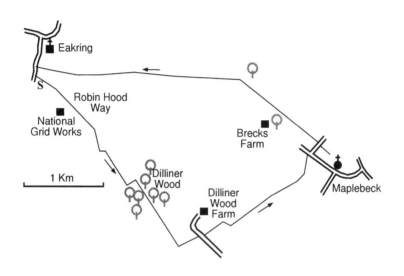

On-street parking is possible at the southern end of Eakring, but please park considerately. To start the walk, go south (heading towards Kirklington) along the road. After passing Pond Farm, turn left along a bridleway signed for the Robin Hood Way. Follow the Way to the north of the National Grid works and then across fields and Mansey Common to reach **Dilliner Wood**.

Walking through Dilliner Wood is enchanting. You will feel, and indeed you are, miles from anywhere. The path through the wood is clearly marked, and, being part of the Robin Hood Way, is well-trodden although not crowded. Coming out of the wood the marked path follows the hedges of fields to reach Orchard Wood Farm, the farm standing on high ground with fine views to the east, towards Lincolnshire.

From the farm, turn left along the farm track, heading north-eastwards to reach the service road for Dilliner Wood Farm. Turn right along the road for 50 yards, then turn left along a signed footpath that follows hedgerows to a stream, The Wink. Cross The Wink by way of a wooden bridge and turn right along a hedge for 100 yards to reach a footpath sign. The sign directs you across a vast field. Walking across this plateau will give you the feeling of being in a very remote situation. Eventually you will see the village of Maplebeck: continue towards it, reaching it at its western end, by the entrance to Brecks Farm.

Turn right and walk downhill into the village. Take the lane next to St Radegund's Church and follow it uphill to its end. Just beyond the entrance to a farm you will see a signpost for a footpath. Take this path, heading north-westwards, behind the village, to reach a country lane. Cross the lane to rejoin the path, which can be seen ahead, crossing another enormous field to reach a patch of woodland that is NOT marked on the OS Landranger map. Aim towards the right side of this wood if ploughing has demolished the path. The path now heads for the left side of the next patch of woodland, one that IS marked on the map.

Beyond this second patch of woodland the path descends to cross a stream (Hagley's Dumble) and is then well-marked as it follows hedgerows back to the village of Eakring. You will enter the village through the playing fields: go along Triumph Road to reach the Kirklington road opposite the Post Office and Stores. A short diversion to the west along a footpath will now bring you to **Mompesson Cross**. Return to the village and follow the Kirklington road back to the start.

POINTS OF INTEREST:

Dilliner Wood – Wildlife abounds in this remote and beautiful coppice.

Mompesson Cross – William Mompesson worked in Eyam between September 1665 and October 1666 during the Great Plague. Three years later he was appointed to the rectorship of Eakring. However, the villagers were so afraid that he might still carry the disease that they made him live for a time in a hut in Rufford Park. The cross marks the spot where Mompesson preached during his exile. Mompesson stayed at Eakring until his death in 1708.

REFRESHMENTS:

The Savile Arms, Eakring.
The Beehive, Maplebeck.

Walk 61   CAUNTON   5¹/₂m (9km)

Maps: OS Sheets Landranger 120; Pathfinder 780.
A walk through wonderfully secluded villages.
Start: At 745601, Main Street, Caunton.

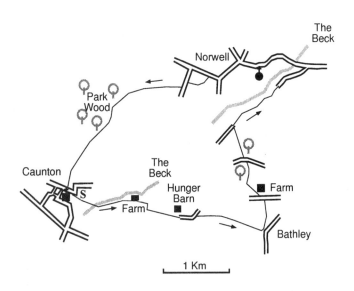

The walk starts on Main Street, between the Plough Inn and St Andrew's Church. Take the footpath eastwards between houses to reach a stream (The Beck). Now continue beside the stream, crossing several fields to reach a concrete bridge over The Beck. Cross and turn left to continue eastwards, following the yellow footpath markers. Pass to the right (south) of some farm buildings, then cross another stream, by way of a wooden bridge. Go across the field beyond, then step through a hedge to reach the end of a track. Turn right and walk through a narrow coppice for 150 yards. Now follow yellow footpath signs out of the coppice into fields. Walk uphill between two fields, passing a solitary oak tree, following a broad, grassy track to Hunger Barn. This residence has magnificent views of the surrounding countryside.

Continue along a footpath heading east towards the village of Bathley. Just before reaching a road close to the village you have a choice. For refreshments, continue ahead, reaching the road and turning right into Bathley. If you do, return to this spot. The route turns left (northwards), following a path through fields to reach a lane. Cross the lane and follow more yellow signs to bypass some farm buildings and a pond. Continue to follow the yellow arrows, crossing more stiles to reach a wood. Go through the wood to reach another lane. Go left for 50 yards, then turn right through a wide hedge and follow the path beyond across several arable fields, aiming for the corner of a patch of woodland. Beyond the woods, go down to reach a path junction in a field. Norwell Church and Windmill are seen in the distance from here. At the junction, take the bridleway going off to the right, following it as it crosses fields and goes close to the banks of The Beck. The bridleway becomes a track: continue along it to reach a lane.

Turn left and follow the lane into the village of Norwell. Walk through the village, passing the Parish Church of St Laurence and the Plough Inn. Leave the village along the Kneesall road, then, at the yellow fire hydrant marker, take the footpath on the left, following it across green fields to reach the Caunton road. Turn left along the road for 100 yards, then take the path on the right. This path leads along the edges of arable fields to reach a green field. Cross this field to Park Wood, reaching the wood at a stile. Do not cross into the wood: instead, turn left and follow the edge of the wood south towards Caunton. Now, do not follow the farm track down to a road: instead, follow a marked path across fields to emerge in the centre of **Caunton**, close to a former non-conformist chapel, now a private dwelling. It is now just a short step back to the start point.

POINTS OF INTEREST:

Caunton – This is a charming village. Samuel Reynolds Hole (Tennyson's 'Rose King') lived in the manor house and was both vicar and squire. Hole loved and studied roses, growing over 400 varieties at Caunton Manor, and promoted exhibitions and societies devoted to roses. Later he became the Dean of Rochester, but was buried in the churchyard at Caunton.

REFRESHMENTS:
The Plough Inn, Caunton.
The Crown, Bathley.
The Plough Inn, Norwell.

Walk 62   **NEWSTEAD ABBEY**   5$\frac{1}{2}$m (9km)

Maps: OS Sheets Landranger 120; Pathfinder 795.

A scenic walk with poetic interest.

Start: At 535509, St Michael's Church, Lindby.

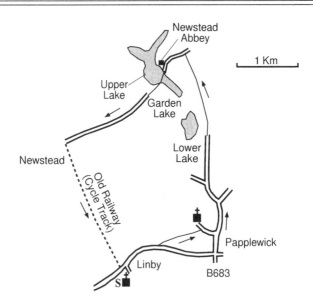

Parking is possible in Church Lane: please park considerately. Walk along Church Lane to reach **Main Street**. Turn right along Main Street, following it through the pretty village of Lindby, heading east towards Papplewick. The Street has charming cottages, two memorial crosses and a maypole. Streams running on both sides add to its attractiveness. On the outskirts of the village there is a gate and footpath sign on the left: take this footpath, following hedges across meadows towards St James' Church, Papplewick.

The path turns left to the church, entering the churchyard through a gate. As you walk through the churchyard, look for the tomb of the Right Honourable Frederick Montague. Leave the church along its driveway to reach the B683. Turn left, along the road (Main Street, Papplewick). There are fine views of Papplewick Hall from the road. After 500 yards Main Street becomes Blidworth Road. At this point take the lane on the left, signed 'Public Footpath to Larch Farm'. The Robin Hood Way also follows this track.

Follow the lane northwards into the Newstead Abbey Estate. As you walk along this tree-lined lane you will be greeted to excellent views of the **Abbey**. When the lane reaches a crossroads, turn left to walk down to the Abbey. It is worth spending time to walk around the wonderful ornamental gardens.

Leave Newstead Abbey by taking the lane which heads south-westwards between Upper Lake and Garden Lake. This tree-lined lane is followed towards the village of Newstead, but before reaching the village, as you leave the Estate, turn left along the cycleway signed for Hucknall. The cycleway was formerly the railway line to the Newstead Colliery. Follow the old track to reach Lindby: St Michael's Church is just to the left.

POINTS OF INTEREST:

Main Street, Lindby – Main Street has two stone crosses and a maypole. The cross nearest to the church has a rare seven-sided base. Damaged by the Puritans in the 1650s, the cross was restored in 1869. The other cross was erected around 1660 to celebrate the restoration of the monarchy. This cross has a stream running under its base.

Newstead Abbey – The abbey was the home of the poet Lord Byron. The original Abbey (actually a priory) was founded by Henry II after the murder of Thomas à Becket. It became the Byron family home after Henry VIII dissolved all of England's monasteries.

REFRESHMENTS:

The Horse and Groom, Lindby.
The White Lady Restaurant, Newstead Abbey.

Walk 63   **HIGH PARK WOOD** $5^1/_2$m (9km)

Maps: OS Sheets Landranger 120 and 129; Pathfinder 795 and 812.

A walk with fine views across north Nottinghamshire and east Derbyshire.

Start: At 484503, a lay-by in the lane to the east of Underwood.

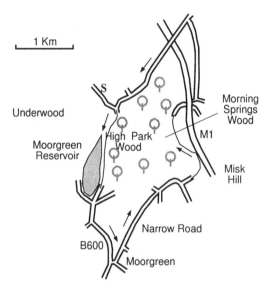

The walk starts at the lay-by at the end of the lane: go past the metal barrier into a small wooded area and continue for 50 yards, then turn right along a footpath. This area has plenty of bird feeders and is very attractive in the spring. Cross a small concrete bridge over a stream and follow blue bridleway signs through the woodland to reach a bridleway junction. Turn right following the signed path for Moorgreen. Follow the well-marked, and well-used, path through High Park Wood, a mixed deciduous and conifer woodland. A rustic fence will help keep you on the right route, though the notices proclaiming shooting in progress look a little tired and, therefore, less authoritative. To the right, through the trees, you will be able to see Moorgreen reservoir. Follow the bridleway to reach the B600 by Beauvale Lodge. Turn left

118

(southwards) towards Moorgreen, following the road, with care, past the Horse and Groom Inn, and then turning left into New Road. Turn left again into Narrow Road (there is a short cut through the car park of the Horse and Groom Inn) and follow it northwards, uphill, with views over High Park Wood, and the remains of **Beauvale Priory**, towards Underwood and Friezelands.

At the top of the hill Narrow Road bends right: continue to the car park, and there, turn left along a bridleway (signed for Annesley and Hucknall), heading north-east towards Misk Hill. Go over a stile and follow the path beside Morning Springs Wood. In the distance the M1 motorway can be both seen and heard. Follow the path to a footbridge over the motorway. Do not cross: instead turn left, following the signs for Annesley, and walk parallel to the motorway to enter Morning Springs Wood. Follow the distinctive yellow waymarkers through the wood to reach a track. Turn right and follow the track as it bends left to reach a cross-tracks. Turn right, heading towards the motorway. When you reach a Y-junction, bear right to go underneath the motorway. On the other side you will reach another Y-junction: bear left, then turn left again after 50 yards. Now follow the footpath signs through a maze of forest tracks: you are always heading northwards, walking parallel to the motorway (with trees between you and it) on its eastern side. On the right, through the hedge, you can see fields. Go through a gate by some houses and continue along the track to reach a T-junction with Weavers Lane.

Turn left along Weavers Lane (a bridleway): there is a sign for America Farm ahead. Follow the bridleway across a footbridge over the motorway to reach open farm land with good views over Nottinghamshire and the remains of Sherwood Forest. Go past America Farm (which is marked on older maps as Newhouse Farm) continuing across high ground and then starting to descend. There are magnificent views over Moorgreen Reservoir and Eastwood from here. The bridleway ceases to be a track and becomes a path, but it is well-used and therefore easy to follow. Felley Priory and the Underwood Church can be clearly seen from the path. Follow the path as it descends to reach a river and the start of the walk.

POINTS OF INTEREST:
Beauvale Priory – This priory was founded in 1343 by Nicholas de Cantelupe, a soldier friend of Edward III. It was the last priory to be founded in England and the first to suffer from Henry VIII's Dissolution of the Monasteries.

REFRESHMENTS:
The Horse and Groom Inn, Moorgreen.

Walk 64   THE PLEASLEY TRAILS   5¹/₂m (9km)

Maps: OS Sheets Landranger 120; Pathfinder 779.

A fine walk along Trails following old mine railways.

Start: At 505642, Pleasley village green. Parking is available at the Pleasley Vale car park at 508648.

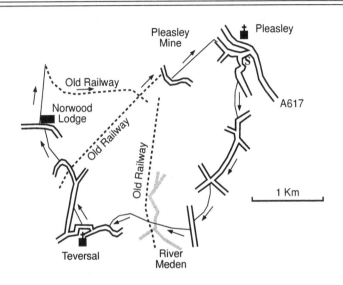

Walk up Crow Hill, opposite the White Swan, the road giving good views across the village. At the crest of the hill there is a footpath sign on the right: take this path, following a line of hawthorns to reach a stile at the corner of a field. Cross into the next field and continue southwards. Go over a stile and clamber down a steep bank to reach a lane (Sampsons Lane) by a bend. Go right to reach the junction with Teminment Lane. Turn left for 50 yards, then turn right along Green Lane, a farm track. Green Lane crosses Top Lane: just to the left of this junction take a footpath on the left. If the field has been ploughed, aim for a derelict brick building. Turn right along a farm track, following it across another field to reach a pair of gates. Cross the stile to the right and go along the edge of the field beyond to reach a lane.

Turn left along the lane for 100 yards, then turn right along a signed, conspicuous green lane beside a field. There are good views as you descend towards the River

Meden and a disused railway line. Go over a stile into a meadow and continue to the narrow concrete bridge crossing the river. Cross the damp meadow beyond to reach a rickety wooden kissing gate. Go through to reach a tunnel under the former railway line. Go through a metal kissing gate and follow yellow arrow waymarkers along a hedgerow, on your right. The footpath reaches a road (Buttery Lane) by a tired metal gate. Turn right and walk into the village of Teversal, soon reaching **St Katherine's Church**. Opposite the church, take the well-used footpath heading north-westwards across fields. Go over a stile on to a country lane and turn right for 350 yards to reach a signed bridleway over a stile on the left. The bridleway, a green lane, crosses another former railway line, then, about 350 yards from the road, makes a sharp left bend: go through the hedge into a field and follow the hedgerow on your left, towards Norwood Lodge.

Step on to a track by the houses and turn left. After about 100 yards, turn right along a path that is, initially, the driveway of Norwood House. Carefully follow the footpath signs through the grounds of Norwood House. At the back of the house the path crosses a field to reach a wood: go through a narrow gap in the fence into the wood and follow a well-marked path through it to reach a river. Cross the river, more of a ditch, and then an arable field to reach another dismantled railway. Turn right along the cinder track, the old railway having been converted into a bridle and cycleway called the Rowthorne Trail. Follow the Trail eastwards for about a mile to reach its end. Go over a stile on to another former railway line (the Teversal Trail) and turn left. Now follow this Trail to its end, a distance of about 350 yards. Go through a gate on to a bridleway and go right to reach the next Trail (after about 200 yards). Turn left and follow this Trail past the remains of **Pleasley Mine** to return to the village of Pleasley.

POINTS OF INTEREST:

St Katherine's Church, Teversal – The church is steeped in history and houses the underground crypt of the Molyneux family. Teversal is also the fictional home of D H Lawrence's controversial novel *Lady Chatterley's Lover*.

Pleasley Mine – Now a ruin, this mine is the subject of a heritage and regeneration project. The surviving chimney and winding towers can be seen from many parts of the walk.

REFRESHMENTS:
The White Swan, Pleasley.
The Nags Head, Pleasley.

Walk 65   **WEST LEAKE HILLS**   5$\frac{1}{2}$m (9km)

Maps: OS Sheets Landranger 129; Pathfinders 833 and 853.

A walk with magnificent Views.

Start: At 536301, the Buttercross, Gotham.

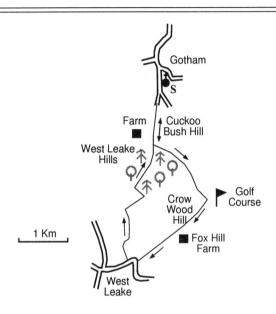

From the Buttercross, between the Sun Inn and **St Lawrence's Church**, walk southwards along Leake Road. Turn right into Hill Road, following the bridleway sign. At the end of the road, go through a metal gate and cross a new road built for British Gypsum. A bridleway sign now directs you uphill through a wooded area and into a steep grassy field.

Climb **Cuckoo Bush Hill** to reach a gate in the hedgerow at the top. Do not go through the gate: instead, turn left and walk along the crest of Court Hill. The path is well-marked and offers excellent views to the east as far as the Vale of Belvoir. Follow the path through a section of woodland to arrive beside a golf course.

The well-maintained path now continues south-eastwards, leaving the golfers to their sport. The excellent views are now to the south-east, to Leicester and Melton Mowbray. Follow the path to a farm track: this is **Crow Wood Hill**. Now turn right (south-westwards) and follow the gently descending path to Fox Hill Farm. The best views are now to the south-west, over Loughborough to Beacon Hill and Bradgate Park in Leicestershire.

At the entrance to Fox Hill Farm a bridleway leaves the track, going between fields downhill towards West Leake. Just before reaching the road the bridleway goes right across a wooden bridge. Now follow the edge of the field as it goes around the back of the houses in West Leake to reach a hedge forming the boundary of the field. Turn left and follow the hedge northwards for 250 yards to reach the next boundary of this large field, by a small wood.

Turn right again and walk eastwards for 150 yards, again following the boundary of the field. Now turn left, northwards, and walk along a broad bridleway to reach a farm lane. Follow the farm lane to a T-junction and turn right (north-eastwards) to follow the lane to the wooded West Leake Hills.

Turn left at the dutch barn at the end of the lane and follow the edge of the wood north-westwards for about 300 yards. A footpath comes in from the left along the boundary of some fields, while on your right there is a bridleway going uphill: turn right and gently climb through the woods, following the well-prepared and well-used bridleway.

Follow the path though the woods to reach a gate. Go through and cross a grassy field to reach another gate at the top of Cuckoo Bush Hill. You have now arrived back to the top of the ridge above Gotham. Go through the gate and reverse the outward route back to the start in Gotham.

POINTS OF INTEREST:
St Lawrence's Church – The church's spire is believed to be one of the oldest stone spires in the country.
Cuckoo Bush Hill – The name derives from a story that the 'Wise Men' of Gotham tried to keep a cuckoo captive by planting a ring of bushes around it.
Crow Wood Hill – The hill is supposedly the site of a Saxon court where the chieftains sat in judgement over the Rushcliffe Hundred.

REFRESHMENTS:
The Sun Inn, Gotham.

Walk 66   **KEYWORTH AND WIDMERPOOL**   5¹/₂m (9km)

Maps: OS Sheets Landranger 129; Pathfinder 834 and 854.

A fine village and beautiful scenery.

Start: At 614308, St Mary Magdalene Church, Keyworth.

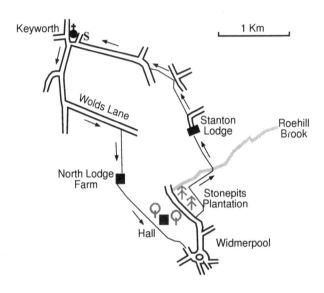

Car parking is available at the village hall in Elm Avenue. From the church, leave Keyworth town centre by walking southwards along Main Street towards Wysall and Wymeswold. At the sharp right turn, continue southwards along Ling's Lane, an unmade lane with some houses on the left and fields beyond a hedge on the right. Follow the lane to a Y-junction.

Bear left along Wolds Lane, from which there are excellent views across the surrounding countryside. Turn right over the first stile and walk beside a hedge (with it on your left), following a well-marked path to North Lodge Farm. Follow the farm track beside a field and go around the farm buildings. Now head south-eastwards across arable fields, heading gently downhill to reach a ditch. Cross the ditch and several more fields to reach the woodland around **Widmerpool Hall**. Walk beside the woodland to reach the drive to the Hall. Continue south-eastwards along the drive to reach the **Church of St Peter and St Paul, Widmerpool**.

After a visit to the church, continue to walk along the drive to reach Fairham Brook. Cross the brook and walk along a footpath to reach a road in an exclusive housing area. This is Church Lane: turn right and walk along it to reach a green triangle. Turn left at the green and walk into the village of Widmerpool.

Turn left at a T-junction and walk along the Keyworth road, passing a road on the right which is heading for the A46 (Foss Way). Continue to reach a signed footpath over a stile on the right. Go over the stile, turn left and walk parallel with the road to reach the Stonepits Plantation. Turn right at the plantation and walk around its boundary, going first north-eastwards and then north-west. At the end of the plantation, continue north-westwards beside a hedge, going downhill to reach Roehill Brook.

Turn right and walk beside the brook for 400 yards, then turn left by a wood and cross the brook. Now walk north-westwards with the wood on your right, keeping to the edge of the fields and passing through a hedge. The path meets the drive for Stanton Lodge (now a nursing home): walk along the drive for 200 yards to where it bends right.

Now go left through a gap in the hedge and head north-westwards across a field. The path is usually well-walked and easy to follow. Cross stiles marked with yellow arrows and go through fields to reach a corral. Enter the corral and turn left, still following the footpath signs, to reach a road. Turn right and follow the road back into Keyworth and the start of the walk.

POINTS OF INTEREST:

Widmerpool Hall – Built in 1873, the Hall was formerly the home of Major Robertson. It is now the national training centre for the AA.

The Church of St Peter and St Paul, Widmerpool – The church has a 14th-century tower hung with bells dated 1592, 1609 and 1612.

REFRESHMENTS:

The Plough Inn, Selby Road, Keyworth.
The Salutation Inn, Main Street, Keyworth.

Walk 67   **BLIDWORTH**   6m (10km)

Maps: OS Sheets Landranger 120; Pathfinder 795.

The homeland of Nottinghamshire's legendary Friar Tuck.

Start: At 588557, in the village of Blidworth.

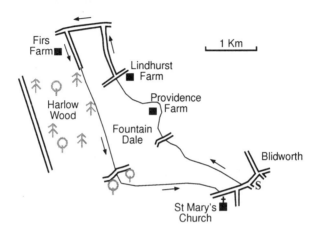

Start opposite the Black Bull Inn, taking the path heading northwards through a small housing estate. Yellow arrows will soon be spotted, leading you across a paddock, and past the backs of more houses to reach steps through a stone wall on to an unmade road. Turn left along the road, passing a children's play and sports area on the left. At a Y-junction, take the bridleway on the left, heading north-west, with a patch of woodland on the right, to reach a cross-paths with a complicated double stile arrangement. Maintain direction, walking along the edge of several grassy fields linked by stiles. Now cross two arable fields (which may be ploughed), going over the brow of a hill in the second.

Go over a stile in a hedge into a grassy field and go diagonally across it to reach a stile on to a lane. Follow the lane to reach a road near Providence Farm. Follow the signed bridleway along the farm track to the farm. Here, signs clearly show you the way around to the right of the buildings. Walk along the edge of a field, then go through a gate into a wood. Follow a well-used track through the wood to reach, at the other side, a crossing bridleway. Maintain direction towards Lindhurst Farm, following a well-defined path across several arable fields. At Lindhurst Farm, go straight across the private road and maintain direction along a bridleway.

Follow the bridleway to reach a road by a housing estate. Turn left and walk along the road for 100 yards to reach a junction. Now follow Old Newark Road, to the left. Once you have passed the estate of flats, the road becomes an unmade bridleway. Follow the bridleway for 700 yards, then turn left (south-eastwards) along another unmade, broad farm track. Walk past the entrance to Firs Farm, on the left, continuing along the track (which is a bridleway) to reach the eastern edge of Harlow Wood. Follow the edge of the wood for 500 yards to reach a crossing track entering the wood from Lindhurst Farm.

Go straight on, continuing along the bridleway for another 500 yards to reach a junction of tracks. Bear right, leaving the edge of the wood, and follow a path through the wood for 500 yards, descending into **Fountain Dale**. Now cross several fields, following a line of telegraph poles to reach a road. Cross the road into woodland and follow a well-defined path for 200 yards to reach its end. Now go left along a path, crossing and going around fields and through meadows (all connected by stiles), heading towards the church at Blidworth. The path becomes enclosed by a holly hedge and a garden fence: continue to reach a final stile and go over on to Rickett Lane. Turn right and walk to the B6020. Cross the road to the **Church of St Mary of the Purification**. Finally, go eastwards along the road, with care, to return to the start.

POINTS OF INTEREST:

Fountain Dale – It is reputed that Friar Tuck had his home in a moated area in this valley. Robin Hood's famous fight on a bridge with Friar Tuck is also supposed to have happened here.

St Mary of the Purification – The unique annual rocking ceremony takes place here every year on the first Sunday in February. The male child born closest to Christmas Day in Blidworth parish is rocked in a flower decked-cradle. This celebrates the presentation of Christ in the Temple. In the churchyard – where Will Scarlet is rumoured to be buried – is a garden of remembrance with a model of the church at its centre.

REFRESHMENTS:
The Black Bull Inn, Blidworth.
The Bird in the Hand, Blidworth.
The White Lion, Blidworth.

Walk 68   **THE MAJOR OAK**   6m (10km)

Maps: OS Sheets Landranger 120; Pathfinder 780.

Nottinghamshire's legendary Sherwood Forest.

Start: At 626675, the car park at the Sherwood Forest Visitor Centre.

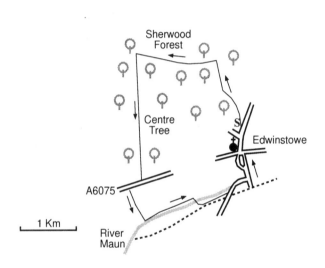

From the car park at the Visitor Centre follow the signs for the **Major Oak**. The path, used by thousands of visitors each year, is very well-defined. There is even a fence to prevent visitors from losing their way.

Continue along the track around the tree and then take the first track on the left. Again the walker will be on a well-defined track. After 320 yards you will reach a junction of tracks: bear right (north-westwards and follow another well-defined track for about 1,100 yards to reach another junction of tracks.

Here, bear left (north-westwards) and follow a track for 400 yards to reach yet another track junction. Turn left (southwards) and follow a well-defined track for 1,100 yards to reach the Centre Tree, another oak. Follow the track straight on, going a little to the right of a pine plantation, for $^3/_4$ mile towards the A6075. Just before

128

reaching the road, the track bears right, running parallel to the road, but just inside the wood. Follow the track for a further 250 yards, then cross the A6075, with care, and head southwards along a bridleway, passing **Archway Lodge** to reach a bridge over the River Maun.

Turn left just before the bridge and go along a bridleway, keeping the river on your right. After about 1,100 yards, turn right and go over two bridges, crossing a flood dyke and the River Maun. Now follow the footpath on the left, keeping the river on your left. Continue along the path to reach a road. Go ahead, along the road into **Edwinstowe**. Turn left along Rufford Road (the B6034), walking through Edwinstowe.

Cross the A6075, again with care, and walk up Church Street, passing **St Mary's Church**. At the boundary of the Country Park you will reach a footpath: follow this path back to the Visitor Centre and its car park.

POINTS OF INTEREST:

Major Oak – This is the largest oak tree in Britain and nowadays is heavily supported by props. Legend has it that Robin Hood and his Merry Men used to hide in it. Originally known as Queen's Oak, it has also been called Cock Pen Oak, as cock fighting once took place beneath it.

Archway Lodge – The Lodge was built in 1842 by the fourth Duke of Portland. In the wall stand figures representing Robin Hood, Little John, Maid Marion, Friar Tuck, Alan-a-Dale and King Richard.

Edwinstowe – The village is named after Edwin, King of Northumbria, who fought a battle nearby in AD632. He was killed in the battle and Edwinstowe grew up around the chapel where his body lay.

St Mary's Church – Legend has it that Robin Hood and Maid Marion were married in this church.

REFRESHMENTS:
The Royal Oak Inn, Edwinstowe.

Walk 69   VICAR WATER   6m (9km)

Maps: OS Sheets Landranger 120; Pathfinder 779 and 780.

A walk with historic and industrial archaeological interest.

Start: At 596629, the Vicar Water car park.

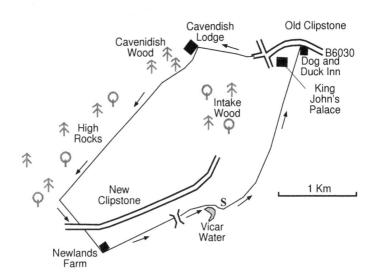

The car park is at the eastern end of Vicar Water. From it, take the bridleway heading eastwards along the banks of the river flowing out of Vicar Water. The blue bridleway signs will guide you on to a track that passes through two tunnels carrying mining workings over the river.

The path continues past mine-workings, on the left, and fields, on the right, indicating the main sources of employment in this area. Continue to follow the blue bridleway signs past a landfill site and then a small industrial complex. Beyond the complex, the path reaches open ground, following the Vicar Water stream northwards.

As you continue along the path, Vicar Water shrinks in stature to little more than a ditch with open grassy fields on both sides. The path eventually enters the car park of the Dog and Duck Inn, in Old Clipstone. On the left, as you reach the inn, you can see the remains of **King John's Palace**.

From the inn, turn left along the B6030, following the pavement into the village of Old Clipstone. Once in the village, take the road on the right, signposted for Warsop, but after about 50 yards, turn left along a lane (Squires Lane) on the left. Follow this metalled lane past a small housing development and then through farmland to reach Cavendish Lodge.

At Cavendish Lodge, Squires Lane bends left (south-westwards) and ceases to be a made road, becoming an unmade bridleway. Continue to follow the lane as it goes past Cavendish Wood. To the left, over Intake wood, you can see the winding towers at Clipstone colliery and the town of New Clipstone. Go through the pedestrian gate beside a locked metal barrier to reach the outskirts of New Clipstone, with the back gardens of houses on your left, and a sports ground on your right.

Turn left and walk down Newlands Drive, passing through a housing estate to reach the B6030. Cross the B6030, with care, and walk down the unmade track immediately opposite. A signpost tells you that Bridleways Guest House and Newlands Farm are both down this lane.

At the Bridleways Guest House, turn left along the footpath beside Vicar Water river. The path becomes a metalled road giving access to the Vicar Water car park: continue along the metalled road (on the northern bank of Vicar Water), passing a metal vehicle barrier. Now go through a tunnel underneath some mine workings. On the other side of the tunnel the stream opens out into a lake: cross a bridge and walk around the edge of the lake to the return to the starting car park. From the end of the lake you will get a good view of the twin winding towers of Clipstone Pit.

POINTS OF INTEREST:

King John's Palace – These are the remains of a palace originally built by the kings of Northumbria and later used by King John as a hunting lodge.

REFRESHMENTS:
The Dog and Duck, Old Clipstone.

Walk 70   **BLYTH**   6m (9km)

Maps: OS Sheets Landranger 120; Pathfinder 744 and 745.

A walk through North Midland farmland.

Start: At 625869, The Green, Blyth.

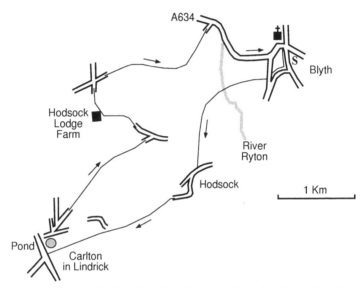

From The Green, opposite the White Swan Inn, turn left and walk southwards along the High Street for a few yards to reach Worksop Road, the B6045. Turn right and walk along the road for 400 yards. Now, just before leaving the village (power lines cross the B6045 at this point), turn right (northwards) along a farm track. From the track there is a good view of the tower of **St Mary and St Martin Church**. After 100 yards, turn left along a broad path heading westwards between two fields and passing under the power lines. From this path there are good views northwards across Blyth to the modern winding tower of Harworth Colliery, and south-westwards to Carlton in Lindrick.

Follow the path to a stile, crossing it and the narrow strip of grassland beyond to reach another stile. Cross and continue to reach the River Ryton. Cross the modern wooden bridge and continue into a small coppice of willows. Follow the well-used path through the coppice, with a hedge on your left. The distinct path leaves the hedge

132

to cross to the corner of an arable field. At the corner, turn left (south-westwards) and follow a broad path, with a hedge on your right. Go through a small coppice to reach a drive. Turn right and walk into the hamlet of **Hodsock**

In the hamlet, turn right along the track heading south-west towards Carlton in Lindrick. Follow this track for $^3/_4$ mile, then, at a right-hand bend in the track, go straight ahead along a footpath, following it across fields and over three stiles to reach the village of Carlton in Lindrick. The path becomes a lane between two stone walls as it reaches a road (The Greenway). Turn right, then, after a few yards, turn left into The Cross which leads into the quaint village centre with its period stone cottages and small green. Those wanting refreshments can call in at the Grey Horses Inn.

Return to The Greenway and turn left, north-west, to reach North Carlton. Turn right into The Green and walk along this charming road to reach the **village pond**. There are several tracks leaving the pond: take the second left, heading north-eastwards. Follow the track, with the tower of Blyth Church on the horizon just to the right, to its end and follow the signed, broad footpath straight ahead, walking with a hedge (and beside it a prepared horse training gallop) on your left.

The path crosses a farm track and becomes a track itself as it continues towards Blyth Church tower. Soon you reach a track running from Hodsock Lodge Farm to Hodsock. Turn left and follow the track to Hodsock Lodge Farm. There, walk through the farmyard, following the signs, and head northwards along a track. After 400 yards you will reach a cross-tracks. Turn right (north-eastwards) and follow a track as it winds its way for nearly $1^1/_4$ miles to reach the A634.

Turn right and follow the broad verge, passing the Charnwood Hotel and then continuing over a bridge to reach the village of Blyth and the start.

POINT OF INTEREST:

St Mary and St Martin Church – The church was founded in 1088.

Hodsock – Early in the spring, the Priory gardens are open to the public for the annual Snowdrop Spectacular. Entry to the five-acre private gardens is through a Grade 1 listed gatehouse, dateing back to the 15th and 16th centuries.

North Carlton Village Pond – The pond was created by local residents. The island is a safe haven for the wildfowl. There are seats and picnic tables around the pond so that residents and visitors can enjoy the scene.

REFRESHMENTS:

The Grey Horses Inn, Carlton in Lindrick.

There are a good choice of places in Blyth, including the Charnwood Hotel which is passed on the route.

Walk 71 **WALESBY** 6m (10km)

Maps: OS Sheets Landranger 120; Pathfinder 763 and 780.
A fine walk through typical North Midland farmland.
Start: At 685708, St Edmund's Church, Walesby.

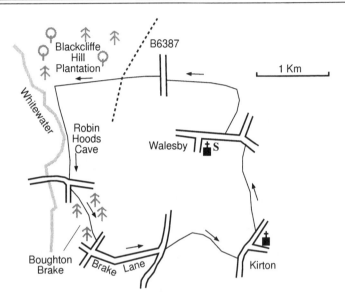

Parking is possible in the village: please park with consideration. From the church with its 15th-century tower, walk eastwards along the road out of the village. Where the road crosses a river (Bevercotes Beck), take the signed footpath on the left, heading north-eastwards beside the beck. Go over a stile in a barbed wire fence into another field, maintaining direction with the beck on your left to reach a wide wooden bridge. Turn left over the bridge and follow a bridleway along the field edges. Cross a green lane and continue to reach the B6387. Turn right (northwards) and follow the hedge beside the road for 130 yards to reach a gap in the hedge. Note that this is different from the route shown on the OS Pathfinder map.

Now cross the road, with care, and follow an alleyway between tall hedges. The path becomes a broad track as it crosses a railway line: continue westwards along the track, keeping the hedge on your right, to reach the Blackcliffe Hill Plantation. Follow the path through the trees to reach a bridleway track. Turn left and walk through open scrub and common beside a stretch of the River Maun known as Whitewater. The path rises above the river as it cuts a bank into a sandstone outcrop. In the bank below the walker is **Robin Hood's Cave**.

Continue along the bridleway to its junction with Whitewater Lane. Cross the road into Boughton Brake, a large patch of woodland, and follow the path going diagonally (south-eastwards) through it, passing a picnic area complete with tables. On leaving the wood, turn left along Brake Lane to reach the B6387. Cross the road, with care, into the field opposite and follow the signed bridleway along a track and into a field. Follow the edge of the field, walking with the hedge on your right. The field narrows into a track: go through a gate then over a stile on the right and follow the path beyond through a farmyard to reach the village of Kirton coming out onto the A6075 opposite the Fox Inn. Turn right to reach refreshments at **Pasture Farm**.

The route turns left along the A6075. At a sharp right-hand bend, continue ahead along a narrow country lane for 450 yards to reach a gate on the left. Go through and enjoy the fine view across fields towards Walesby. Now go diagonally across the grassy field and, at the far corner, go through a pair of gates either side of a bridge. Take a broad farm track northwards and, at its end, follow footpath signs along the edge of a grassy field, walking with a hedge on your right to reach a stile. Go over into an arable field and follow the signed footpath along the edge of the field to reach a green lane. Follow the lane to a junction of country roads on the outskirts of Walesby. There is even a seat here, in memory Wilf Fillingham, for the weary walker to rest on. Turn left along the lane to return to Walesby.

POINTS OF INTEREST:

Robin Hood's Cave – The caves are minor hollows in a steep bank above the Whitewater section of the River Maun. The caves are an attraction to the occupants of the nearby Scout Camp, though it is most unlikely that they were ever a serious habitat for Robin Hood.

Pasture Farm – This farm guest house and tea room offers horse-drawn carriage rides. There is also a museum of carriages and other memorabilia.

REFRESHMENTS:
The Fox Inn, Kirton.
The Red Lion, Walesby.
The Carpenters Arms, Walesby.

Walk 72   **TEVERSAL**   6m (10km)

Maps: OS Sheets Landranger 120; Pathfinder 779.

A walk through typical North Midlands farm scenery.

Start: At 479613, the Teversal Visitor Centre.

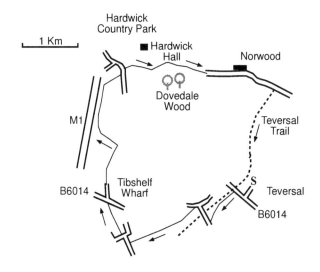

From the Visitor Centre, walk back along Carnarvon Street to the B6014. Turn right and follow the road, with care, towards the railway bridge. Turn left at the bridge and follow the footpath that runs parallel to the railway line. Go through a farmyard, then follow the yellow footpath signs through fields linked by gates. After the second field the path leaves the railway and goes diagonally across two grassy fields. When the path reaches a farm lane, turn right along the lane, heading back towards the railway line. Cross the railway, with care, at a level crossing and continue along the lane. Now go to the left of the houses, following a yellow arrow through the hedge on the left. Turn left at the corner of the field and walk with the hedge to your right to reach a crossing of paths. Take the middle route, heading west(-ish) along a line of fencing.

Follow the footpath across three fields to reach a farm. Now be careful to follow the vague footpath signs to the left (heading southwards) of the farm buildings to reach a country lane.

Turn right and follow the lane to a T-junction. Go left for 50 yards, then turn right along a signed footpath. There are excellent views from this point. Follow the footpath across fields linked by stiles, yellow waymarkers showing the way. The path emerges from an alley between gardens at Tibshelf Wharf on to the B6014: cross the road, with care, and walk along Wharf Lane (a bridleway) beside Wharf Cottage. Follow the bridleway to a junction of paths by a gate and stile. Take the path that goes diagonally across a field, aiming for **Hardwick Hall**. As the footpath ascends a hill, Hardwick Hall disappears from view: continue to reach a junction of paths by a gate and stream. Go left, uphill, crossing the brow of the hill. Hardwick Hall now returns to view. The path now descends towards the M1 motorway, following the embankment northwards by a stream. Cross another stream by way of a weir, and turn right along the field edges, walking with the hedgerow and stream to your right. Go over a stile on to a country lane opposite a car park for Hardwick Hall.

Cross the lane and walk through the car park to reach the Hardwick Inn. Now stroll up the drive (the sign saying 'No Entry' refers to cars), and, when it bends left around sandstone cliffs, take the footpath to the right, heading eastwards through open parkland to reach the top of Dovedale Wood. Cross a stile on to a track and bear right, eastwards, through shady woodland. At the end of the woodland the track reaches a gate: go through on to a lane (Newbound Lane). Bear left along the lane, following it through open countryside with views across to Teversal.

Follow Newbound Lane past Norwood Lodge to reach a disused railway line, the Teversal Trail. Turn right along the cinder track. This former railway has been converted into a bridle and cycleway now called the Teversal Trail: follow the Trail back to the Visitor Centre.

POINTS OF INTEREST:

Hardwick Hall – Although strictly in Derbyshire a visit is well worthwhile. The Hall is the former home of Bess of Hardwick, a lady who had much influence over the nearby Dukeries estates.

REFRESHMENTS:

The Hardwick Inn, Hardwick Hall.
Teversal Grange Country Inn, Teversal Visitor Centre.

Walk 73 CHURCH WARSOP 6m (10km)

Maps: OS Sheets Landranger 120; Pathfinder 779.

North Midland scenery and a delightful village.

Start: At 568687, the Church of St Peter and St Paul, Church Warsop.

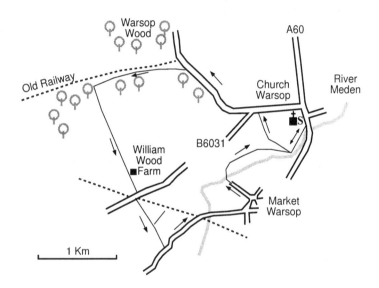

From the church car park, follow the bank of the River Meden south-west, passing fishermen along the way. By a footbridge turn right, away from the river, and follow a footpath across the green towards a children's play area. Go through an old iron kissing gate and follow the broad path beyond across a field. At a T-junction of tracks, turn right to walk along the edge of a field to reach the B6031 at its junction with Wood Lane.

Cross the B6031, with care, and walk along Wood Lane, passing playing fields on your left. Follow Wood Lane as it leaves the village of Church Warsop, continuing along it to reach the remains of a railway bridge. Close to the old bridge, turn left along a bridleway which will shortly bring you on to a cinder track that follows the line of the old trackbed. Bear left (westwards) along the track, following it through Warsop Wood. Follow the track for about $^3/_4$ mile to reach an obvious track, much used by horses, on the left.

Descend the steep bank and walk along the track, which runs beside a regenerating slag heap, to reach William Wood Farm, passing the grounds of Basset Model Flying Club. Continue along the bridleway, which becomes a concrete track as it passes the remains of the mine at Warsop Vale. The right of way passes the gardens of terraced houses as it approaches the railway bridge crossing the B6031.

Pass beneath the railway bridge and take the signed track to the left. Follow the track (Spring Lane) between fields. The track becomes a narrow path: continue along it to emerge on to Sookholme Lane beside beautiful Herring Cottage. Turn left in front of the cottage and follow Sookholme Lane under a railway arch to reach the outskirts of Market Warsop.

Turn left into The Hawthorns and follow it to Stonebridge Lane. Turn left again, following Stonebridge Lane to the River Meden. Cross the bridge over the river and turn right to follow the footpath through hawthorn bushes to reach fields. Now walk between the fields, with the church and **Rectory** at Church Warsop straight ahead. Finally, follow the path back to the children's play area and the car park at Church Warsop.

POINTS OF INTEREST:
The Rectory, Church Warsop – The Rectory, which is part Tudor, was originally the home of the Fitzherberts.

REFRESHMENTS:
None on the route, though there are several possibilities just off the route in Market Warsop.

Walk 74   CHURCH WARSOP AND CUCKNEY   6m (10km)

Maps: OS Sheets Landranger 120; Pathfinder 779.

A fine walk linking two delightful villages.

Start: At 568687, the Church of St Peter and St Paul, Church Warsop.

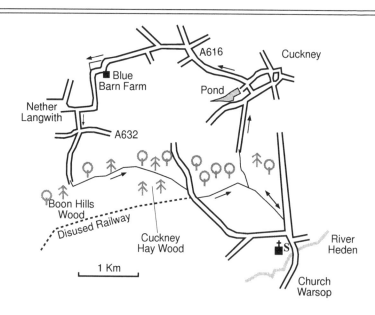

From the church car park, walk northwards along the broad pavement beside the A60, passing the church and its **Rectory**. Cross the B6031, with care, and continue along the A60 for another 100 yards to reach a signed footpath on the left just as you leave the village. Cross an arable field, heading towards a wood. Go over a stile and follow the well-used footpath across three fields to reach the corner of Cuckney Hay Wood.

At the corner of the wood, step through a gap in the hedge and follow a broad track north-eastwards beside the wood to reach a cross-tracks. Continue straight on, heading more northwards now, and going through mixed woodland. The path leaves the woodland to reach a track by Park House Farm. Turn left, and then right to follow the track towards the hamlet of Cuckney.

Cross the A632, with great care, to reach a footpath. Go over a pair of stiles and climb a bank. At the top of the knoll you will get your first glimpse of the mill pond at Cuckney. The path descends into the hamlet. Cross the end of the pond by the former mill, now a primary school, and follow the footpath around the pond to reach the sluice gates. Turn right and follow the hedge on your right through a field to reach the A616.

Turn left along the A616, a broad grass verge giving you a safe area on which to walk. At the main road's junction with a pair of country lanes, continue along the A616. Now, take the next lane on the left towards Blue Barn Farm, a footpath sign indicating the way. Go along the lane, but bypass the farm by following the footpath signs around two sides of a field. Leave the field to rejoin the lane, heading south along it towards Nether Langwith.

The lane makes a sharp right turn and then reaches Limes Avenue: turn left and walk along the pavement into Nether Langwith. Cross the A632, with great care, and walk down the bridleway opposite the Jug and Glass Inn. Walk through a farmyard and continue along the track as it gently climbs to Boon Hills Wood. There are good views from this track.

Follow the track as it turns left to go through the narrow strip of woodland. At the top of the hill a path leaves the track, going over a stile to continue through Boon Hills Wood. Take this, following it to reach a choice of paths. Go left, then right, heading north-eastwards along the ridge line, with a hedge on your right and fields to your left. Now cross a track to enter Cuckney Hay Wood and follow the well-used and well-marked path through the wood. In the right season the wood is carpeted with bluebells.

When you reach a country lane by the dismantled bridge of a former railway line, cross the lane and walk along the track that follows the edge of the woods, heading eastwards at first, then north-eastwards. Follow the track to reach the cross-tracks met at the beginning of the walk. Turn right and reverse the outward route, enjoying the excellent views across north Nottinghamshire.

POINTS OF INTEREST:
The Rectory, Church Warsop – The Rectory, which is part Tudor, was originally the home of the Fitzherberts.

REFRESHMENTS:
The Jug and Glass, Nether Langwith.

Walk 75   **BUNNY AND GOTHAM**   6m (10km)

Maps: OS Sheets Landranger 129; Pathfinder 853.

A walk with magnificent views.

Start: At 583296, St Mary the Virgin Church, Bunny.

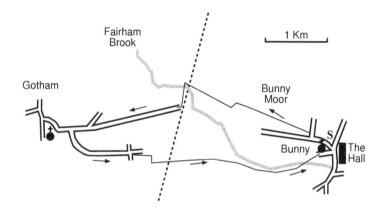

Parking is available - with care and consideration - in Church Street, Bunny outside the **Church of St Mary the Virgin**. Walk along Church Street to Moor Lane and, at the end of Moor Lane, turn right (northwards) along a farm track. After 100 yards, turn left along another farm track. This track becomes an alley between hedges and then reduces to a footpath leading east-north-eastwards beside a ditch.

Turn left at a footbridge and head south-westwards for 25 yards to reach a broad greenswarth. Now turn right and walk along this greenswarth, heading north-west across Bunny Moor towards the Great Central (Nottingham) railway line. As you near the railway line the track reduces to a path. Stiles guide you across the railway. Currently the railway is not in use but the Great Central (Nottingham) Railways hope eventually to use this line as a connection between themselves and Loughborough. When that happens walkers will need to take great care when crossing.

Once across the railway, turn left and walk along a broad farm track beside the railway, heading south towards a wood. At the wood the track bends right: the track is Moor Lane and can be followed all the way to the Sun Inn in Gotham. However, the return route turns off Moor Lane, using the bridleway (on the left as you approach the village).

If you visit the village, return along Moor Lane and turn right along the signed bridleway, following a lane south-south-eastwards. After 300 yards the lane bends left: continue along it, following the bridleway signs. Eventually the lane reaches a crossing track. Again you follow the bridleway signs, turning right to cross a bridge and then going left to walk beside a field, with a narrow wooded area on your left.

Follow the field boundary rightwards to reach a large wooden bridge. After a further 200 yards you will reach a wide wooden bridge on the left. Cross the bridge and continue along the edge of a field to reach the railway embankment. Now turn left through a wooden gate to reach a tunnel under the railway line.

Go under the railway and continue eastwards, following a bridleway between fields. When the bridleway branches right, maintain direction across arable fields to reach Fairham Brook. Now follow a broad and well-used path along the southern bank of the brook. The spire of the church and the tower of Bunny Hall now dominate the view, acting as signposts. Follow the path through a couple of hedges at the boundaries of fields, and continue to reach a large and well-made bridge on the left. Cross the bridge and walk north-eastwards across one last field to reach Main Street, Bunny.

POINTS OF INTEREST:

The Church of St Mary the Virgin, Bunny – The church is known as The Cathedral of the Wolds. Inside there is a life size monument of Sir Thomas Parkyns in a wrestling stance. In 1712 Sir Thomas established an annual Midsummer Day wrestling match in the village. Many of the original buildings in this village were designed by Sir Thomas who lived in Bunny Hall and was also an amateur architect.

REFRESHMENTS:
The Sun Inn, Gotham.
The Cuckoo Bush, Gotham.
The Rancliffe Arms, Bunny.

Walk 76   **ATTENBOROUGH**   6m (10km)

Maps: OS Sheets Landranger 129; Pathfinder 833.
A walk through a fine wetlands Nature Reserve.
Start: At 515339, the Nature Reserve car park.

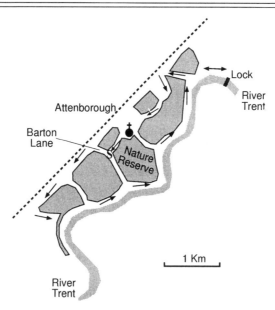

The car park - in Barton Lane, Attenborough - is on an island in the middle of a former gravel pit, now a **Nature Reserve**. From it, walk back along Barton Lane to the railway level crossing. There, turn left, south-westwards, along the unmade track beside the railway. The railway carries Nottingham to London Intercity trains as well as regional trains to Derby and further west. The line is on your right: to the left are the Nature Reserve lakes, while ahead are the cooling towers of the Ratcliffe-on-Soar Power Station. Cross a wooden bridge with a low metal barrier over the River Erewash. The track now briefly leaves the railway, passing through a wooded area before rejoining the railway at another level crossing. Turn right and walk along the top of an embankment, with an arable field to the left and a grassy paddock to the right. After 400 yards the path splits: to the right the path continues along the embankment to reach some picnic tables. Our route goes left, descending from the embankment and

144

passing between wooden posts to go along a prepared track. Follow the track through Willow trees, and past a bridge to reach the banks of the River Trent by fishing marker number 65. Turn left and walk along the narrow strip of land separating the river from the Nature Reserve. The Trent, with its boats and fishermen, is to your right, the Nature Reserve is to your left. Across the river you will see various moored narrow boats and a number of weekend homes close to the water.

The prepared path is well-used: follow it as it makes its way between the Trent and the Nature Reserve. To the right, across the river, is the village of Barton in Fabis with Gotham Hill behind. Mill Hill hides Clifton. Cross an outflow from the Nature Reserve by a couple of houses. At this point you can turn left to return to the car park. The route bears right to continue along the Trent's bank. The river now goes around a significant bend before reaching the next opportunity to shorten the route. At the next outflow you can turn left to reach Attenborough. The route continues along the riverbank. On this stretch of the river there is plenty of activity from the local Sailing Club. Continue along the path to reach **Beeston Marina and Beeston Lock**.

Now return along the river for 300 yards to reach an obvious track going right. Follow this prepared track through the Nature Reserve, going between ponds and heading towards the railway line. At the railway, turn left and follow the path through mixed woodland and an area of scrub to reach a high metal and wood bridge. Cross on to an island and walk along the track to the outskirts of Attenborough. Now follow a tarmac drive (The Strand) through the **Attenborough Village Conservation Area**, passing the bowling green and cricket pitch. Turn left into Church Lane and then take the footpath signed for Barton Ferry Lane. Start along the drive to Ireton House, which stands beside St Mary's Church. Follow the footpath back to the Nature Reserve, then follow the prepared path between the ponds back to return to the car park.

POINTS OF INTEREST:

Nature Reserve – Opened in 1966, this extensive Wetlands Reserve is a former sand and gravel quarry.

Beeston Marina and Lock – There will be much boating activity for you to watch here. The lock is where Beeston Canal starts. This canal later becomes the Nottingham Canal as it makes its way through Castle Marina to the centre of Nottingham.

Attenborough Village Conservation Area – The origins of Attenborough goes back to Saxon times when the settlement was called *Adenburgh* meaning Ada's town.

REFRESHMENTS:

The Riverside Bar, Beeston Marina.

Walk 77   **VALE OF BELVOIR**   6m (10km)

Maps: OS Sheets Landranger 129; Pathfinder 834.

A walk through the beautiful Belvoir Vale.

Start: At 751362, Granby Church.

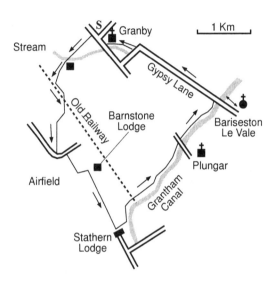

Please park with care and consideration in the village. Walk along Church Street, passing both the village inns, then turn left at Granby Motors and walk along a track to reach a stile. Go over and follow a path across a grass field to reach a stream and another grass field. Follow the stream to Station Farm, then cross it by footbridge and bear right to cross a wide grass verge, in front of Station Farm, to reach a gate in a hedge. Go through and follow the left hedge of the grassy field beyond to reach another gate. Turn right and walk to a third gate. Follow the track beyond to reach a disused railway. Turn left along the old trackbed for 250 yards, with views across the Vale of Belvoir to Belvoir Castle. Now just before reaching a wooden barrier across the track, turn right and descend the bank to reach a footbridge across a ditch. The path beyond goes south-west beside the perimeter fence of a former quarry to reach another footbridge. Cross into a grassy field and go diagonally across to reach the far corner.

Now follow the footpath for a few yards to reach the perimeter of Langar Airfield. This is an active airfield and home of the local parachute club, so the walker may well see light aircraft taking off or landing, and the skies may be full of colourful parachutes. Turn left and walk along the perimeter track towards Barnstone Lodge. Just before reaching the Lodge, turn right along a bridleway (a concrete track), following it south-eastwards.

Just before reaching the end of the track, turn left and follow the hedge beside an arable field. Turn right to cross a ditch and follow the edge of another arable field to reach another concrete road. At the end of this road, turn right, and then left, to follow a bridleway to Stathern Lodge.

At the Lodge, a former farm, turn left and walk past a cottage to pick up a track heading north-eastwards across arable fields, heading towards an obvious yellow marker and the Grantham Canal. Turn left and stroll along the beautiful towpath, with its abundance of wildlife. Signs along the towpath stating the distance from the River Trent indicate the former commercial importance of the canal. Those wanting refreshments, or maybe just to explore the village of Plungar, should go over the bridge reached after about $1\frac{1}{2}$ miles. The walk continues along the canal towpath as far as bridge No. 50 and Gypsy Lane.

For an excellent view across the Vale of Belvoir you should now take a short diversion, about 300 yards south-eastwards along the lane to a **Trig. Point** beside the road to Barkestone-le-Vale. After taking in the view, return to the Grantham Canal and continue along Gypsy Lane. The lane bends sharp left about $1\frac{1}{4}$ miles from the trig. point. Follow the lane around the bend and then take a footpath on the right, through a gap in the hedge. Go left to follow Rundle Beck to a footbridge. Cross the bridge into a field and follow a hedge to a road. Turn right and follow the road for the final 200 yards back into Granby and the start of the walk.

POINTS OF INTEREST:
Trig. Point – As would be expected of all Ordnance Survey triangulation points this spot offers excellent views, here across the Vale of Belvoir.

REFRESHMENTS:
The Marquis of Granby, Granby.
The Boot and Shoe, Granby.
The Belvoir Inn, Plungar.

Walk 78   **E**ASTWOOD   6m (10km)

Maps: OS Sheets Landranger 129; Pathfinder 812.
A longer walk through D H Lawrence country.
Start: At 465485, the Brinsley Picnic Site car park.

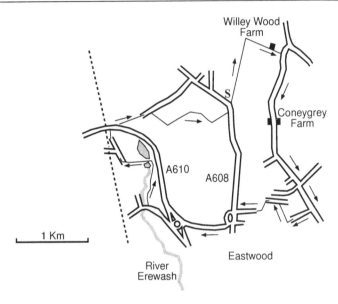

From the car park, take the footpath heading northwards, going through a wooden gate and along a dismantled railway line. Go left to look at the monument of **Brinsley Pit**. Return to the prepared path along the old, tree-lined trackbed and follow it through a wood. Continue along the trackbed to reach another path crossing under the track. Now go right and descend steps to that path. Go over a stile and continue through grassy fields to reach Willey Wood Farm. The path crosses the entrance to the farmyard. This entrance is used by cows twice daily to be milked and, after rain, you will realise that, compared with cows, pigs get a bad press.

Continue through a field to reach a track. Turn right and follow it as it descends a ridge. From here there are excellent views to the east, south and west. Continue to walk south along the bridleway towards Eastwood, which you can clearly see across the valley. Follow the footpath signs around Coneygrey Farm and back on to the bridleway track. Continue along the track to reach a road (Lower Beau Vale) on the outskirts of Eastwood. Turn right and then left to walk up Mill Road. Turn right into Walker Street and follow it to **The Canyons**. Walk through The Canyons to reach Garden Road. You are now on the **Blue Line Trail**. Turn left to pass 28 Garden Road, one of the Lawrence family's homes. Continue along Garden Road, following the blue line painted on the pavement as it goes left into an alley and then leads through Atherfield Gardens to Princes Street. Turn left and walk up Victoria Street to the D H Lawrence Birthplace Museum.

Continue up Victoria Street to reach Nottingham Road. Turn right and walk to a major junction. Cross, with care, and continue westwards along Derby Road (the A608). Follow the footpath across the junction with the A610 and continue along Derby Road towards the Erewash Canal. Go past the canal and turn right beside the Mill Inn to follow a footpath northwards through waste ground, walking beside the River Erewash. Follow the footpath across open ground and over the river to reach Comford Road.

Turn right along Comford Road to reach Plumptre Road. Follow the road to reach Plumptre Farm and an unmade track passing beneath the A610 beside a railway line. Follow the track as it bends right to, briefly, follow the A610 and then goes through marshy land towards Brinsley. The surface changes to tarmac as the track starts up a steep hill. Now take the bridleway sign opposite a house no. 100, following the prepared track – with good views to Brinsley and Eastwood – over the former spoil heap and down to the car park.

POINTS OF INTEREST:
Brinsley Pit – These wooden headstocks are a tribute to the old Brinsley Pit that once occupied the site.
The Canyons – In D H Lawrence's time this was open ground and cornfields.
Blue Line Trail – The blue line trail guides visitors to various important places in the life of D H Lawrence.

REFRESHMENTS:
The Brinsley Lodge, Brinsley.
The Great Northern, Derby Road, Langley Mill.
The White Peacock Tea Shop, Victoria Street, Eastwood.

Walks 79 & 80   **ROBIN HOOD HILL**   7m (12km)
or 9m (15km)

Maps: OS Landranger 120; Pathfinder 796.
Magnificent views.
Start: At 675542, Radley Road, Halam.

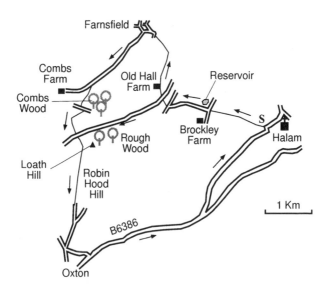

The walk starts at a Z-bend in Radley Road, the road from Oxton to Halam. Follow the footpath heading west-north-westwards across a field, passing Manor House and going through a small wood. Cross a stream over a concrete bridge and follow yellow footpath signs gently uphill through several hedges. Follow the path to a junction of tracks by a small reservoir. Maintain direction along track rising to reach a T-junction. Go left for 25 yards, then take the path on the right, going over a stile and descending steeply to reach a farmyard and a narrow country lane.

    The shorter walk turns left here, following the lane for $1\frac{1}{4}$ miles, passing Rough Wood, on the left, and rejoining the longer route at a track, also to the left, just beyond.

The longer walk crosses the lane, and the meadow beyond, heading towards Old Hall Farm, its house painted in a distinctive pink wash. The path around this farm house can be indistinct, but with care it can be followed to reach the fields on the other side. Yellow arrows now show the way to Cotton Mill Farm, where peacocks provide decoration. Cross a track then follow the yellow arrows along field edges towards Farnsfield. Go through the Acres Recreation Ground, then behind some houses to emerge by the car park for the Warwick Arms Inn, in Tippings Lane. Walk south along Tippings Lane to reach its junction with Quaker Lane and Combs Lane. Go along Combs Lane for a mile to reach a footpath sign, on the right, for the Robin Hood Way. Follow the Way south-westwards across a field, heading towards Combs Wood. The path through the wood is well-marked: exit the wood on to a track and turn left, uphill, along it for 100 yards. Now go right, through the hedge, and right again to follow the hedgerow westwards towards Oxton Grange, at present out of sight. A lonely signpost by an equally lonely oak tree indicates a change of direction. You can now see Robin Hood Hill beyond a country lane: descend to the lane. The shorter route rejoins here.

Head south-eastwards along the track from the lane to reach a left-hand bend. Here a path crosses a narrow strip of field on the right: follow this path to the corner of the wood on Loath Hill. Follow the right (western) edge of the wood to a fence. This fence marks the boundary of the **Robin Hood Hill** encampment, managed by English Heritage. Cross the stile into the encampment and bear left to climb to the top of the hill. Follow the ridge down to reach the fence again. Cross a stile and go along the well-used path towards Oxton. The path becomes a track which in turn becomes a road: walk along Blind Lane to reach the B6386. Turn left, with care, and follow the road for $1\frac{1}{2}$ miles to reach a lane, on the left, for Halam. Follow this lane as it descends into the charming village of Halam.

POINTS OF INTEREST:

Robin Hood Hill – The precise history of the encampment on the hill is unknown. However, it is believed that it was the original settlement for what became Oxton. The views from the site are tremendous. On a good day you can see across Nottinghamshire into Derbyshire, Leicestershire and Lincolnshire.

REFRESHMENTS:

The Wagon and Horses, Halam.
The Warwick Arms, Farnsfield.
The Green Dragon, Oxton.

Walk 81   **RUFFORD**   7m (11km)

Maps: OS Sheets Landranger 120; Pathfinder 780.

A walk through one of Nottinghamshire's great estates.

Start: At 668665, Wellow Pond car park.

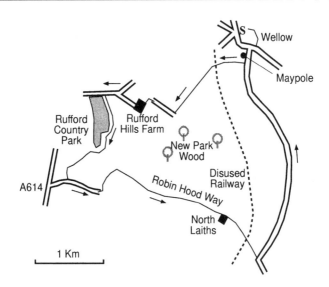

From the car park, walk eastwards along the lane behind the houses of Wellow village, then along a track into the car park and beer garden of the Durham Ox Inn. Cross the A616, with care, and walk along the Eakring road to reach the **maypole**. Continue along the Eakring road, leaving Wellow and soon crossing a little river. Now take the signed footpath, to the right, into the playing fields. Follow the hedge on the left around the edge of the playing fields to reach a stile. This and a twin stile, both with yellow arrows, lead you into and across two paddocks to reach a track beside a disused railway line. The track is now a horse gallop. Cross the gallop and descend the steep embankment to reach the disused railway line. Although the embankment is steep there are steps to aid the walker. Cross the old railway track and ascend the opposite embankment, again aided by steps. Cross another gallop track to reach a footpath sign.

Cross a field heading south-westwards. As the ground here is convex, your destination is out of view. You will soon reach a track that is not marked on the OS Landranger map. Cross this track and maintain direction across another field. In this field you will see a solitary holly tree: aim for this tree if the path has disappeared under the plough. When you reach a farm track, turn right and follow it to Rufford Hills Farm.

Follow a path south-westwards, then north-westwards, around the farm buildings, continuing along a track to reach a road, turn left and follow the road for 100 yards, then take the footpath, on the left, leading into the Rufford Country Park. The path goes around a lake and into the ruined **abbey** complex. Continue past a penned area for Mouflon sheep. These sheep are the ancestors of the present day domesticated sheep. In the woods near the sheep there is an animal graveyard.

Now, near the Craft Centre, go through a gate in the high brick wall to reach a gravel drive behind the Orangery. Walk along the drive to reach a road at a triangular green with a seat. Turn left and walk eastwards along the road. This section of the route is part of Robin Hood Way.

Follow the road into Rufford Golf Course. Turn left and walk along a track to reach a bridge over a stream. Cross and, by the tee for the 16th hole, turn right and walk along a track towards North Laiths Farm. At the farm you leave Robin Hood Way, continuing south-eastwards along a track to reach a road (the Eakring road from Wellow).

Turn left and follow the road back to Wellow. This fine country lane has a wide verge which will keep you away from the sparse traffic and offers extensive views. From Wellow, reverse the first part of the walk to return to the start.

POINTS OF INTEREST:

Wellow Maypole – Wellow is a conservation village. The permanent maypole is well known and attracts visitors from far and wide for the traditional crowning of the May Queen, a ceremony which goes back centuries.

Rufford Abbey – The abbey has an interesting history. It was founded in the 12th century by Gilbert de Gaunt. After the Dissolution it was given to the Earl of Shrewsbury. The Earl's daughter-in-law, Bess of Hardwick, built the Elizabethan House.

REFRESHMENTS:
The Coach House, Rufford Abbey.
The Durham Ox, Wellow.
The Olde Red Lion, Wellow.

Walk 82   **FLINTHAM WOOD**   7m (11km)

Maps: OS Sheets Landranger 129 (and 120, but only for a few yards); Pathfinder 813.

Good walking, with magnificent views over the River Trent.

Start: At 759479, All Saints' Church, Elston.

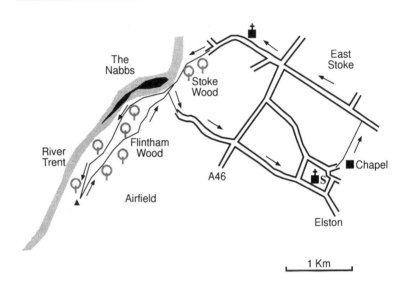

Go north along the footpath beside the church, then walk around the village playing field and take the path at the far end to reach Low Street. Turn left, and then right into Old Chapel Lane. At the end of the lane, go through a kissing gate into a grassy field. **Old Elston Chapel** is in this field. Cross the field and go through another kissing gate into another field. Turn left and walk through the field, passing a commemorative Chestnut Tree. Go though Stoke Fields Farm yard and follow the farm drive to Moor Lane. Turn left and walk along Moor Lane to East Stoke. Moor Lane reaches the A46 (Foss Way): cross this main road, with great care, and walk down School Lane. Pretty red-brick cottages line this road. Leave the village and continue down the lane, which is now called Church Lane. On the right is a high rustic brick wall bounding the parkland of Stoke Hall. St Oswald's Church is on the right next to the entrance to Stoke Hall. The lane bends to the left: to the right you can see the villages of Morton and Rolleston on the other side of the Trent. The lane makes a sharp right turn. Here, maintain direction along a green lane. Stoke Wood is on your left, while to the right there are grassy fields with the River Trent beyond them. The lane diminishes to a footpath: continue along it, crossing grassy fields to reach the bank of the River Trent. In the river you will see The Nabbs, an island which splits the river in two. On your side is a weir, while out of view on the other side there is a lock.

Walk along the broad grassy plain that is the riverbank to reach Flintham Wood. Now go up the tree-clothed and steep hillside to reach a gate. Go through and continue uphill over grassy heathland to reach the boundary of **Syerston Airfield**. The map shows an Ordnance Survey **trig. point** at the high point of this hill.

Now turn around and walk, through the heathland, heading north-north-eastwards to reach a track at the eastern end of Flintham Wood. Go through a wooden gate and walk along the lane beyond to reach a junction. Turn left (northwards) and follow the lane down to the riverside meadows. Turn right and walk along the path for 500 yards to reach a green lane on the right. Turn right and follow the lane (Trent Lane) gently uphill through farmland. From the high point you will be able to see over Elston and the River Devon valley into the Vale of Belvoir. The track then gently descends to reach a gate. Go through to reach the A46 (Foss Way) at a lay-by.

Cross, with great care, and walk along Lodge Lane into the village of Elston. Lodge Lane becomes Top Street: follow this back to the start.

POINTS OF INTEREST:
Old Elston Chapel – The chapel has a Norman doorway. It is now maintained by the Redundant Churches Fund.
Syerston Airfield – This airstrip is used as a glider pilot training centre. In good weather walkers will see gliders taking off to fly over the river Trent.
Trig. Point – The trig. point has disappeared but the truly magnificent view remains. Across the River Trent, Nottinghamshire is laid out as if it were a map. Time spent here identifying notable landmarks such as Nottingham itself, Southwell Minster and Newark will be well spent.

REFRESHMENTS:
The Chequers Inn, Toad Lane, Elston.
The Pauncefote Arms, Moor Lane, East Stoke.

Walk 83   **HOLME**   7¹/₂m (13km)

Maps: OS Sheets Landranger 121; Pathfinder 764.

A walk along the River Trent, visiting an interesting hamlet.

Start: At 827613, The Green, Collingham.

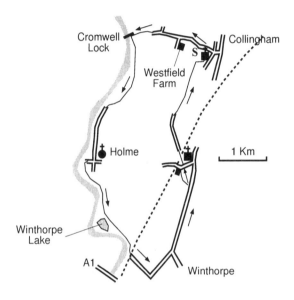

Walk westwards along The Green with its pretty red-brick houses to reach Stocks Hill, and then go along Westfield Lane by a signpost for the River Trent. All Saints' Church will be on your left. The tarmac road turns left into Westfield Farm. Do not turn with it: instead, go straight on, heading westwards along a bridleway, following the signpost for the River Trent. On this section of the route, as you approach the river, you will be walking through a typical rich flood plain. You arrive at the river by walking through an angler's car park: turn left, go over a stile and walk along the raised east bank of the River Trent, heading towards the village of Holme. On the opposite bank is Cromwell Lock.

    This section of the walk is part of the Trent Valley Way. The raised bank gives good views over the river towards some quarry works and the farmland beyond. The path, and the raised bank, soon leave the river and makes its way through open farmland.

Cross a bridge over a brook, continuing across the grassy field beyond, heading towards the River Trent to join a farm track. Follow this track towards the village of **Holme**.

You may go through the village if you wish: St Giles' Church is certainly worth a look. But there is an alternative, the path going around the western side of the village. Either way you will rejoin the Trent Valley Way on the south side of the village. Continue along the Way, passing through gentle farmland, then passing Winthorpe Lake before reaching a road by a level crossing for the main Nottingham to Lincoln railway line. Bear right, going over the level crossing with care, and follow the road into Winthorpe.

At a crossroads opposite the Lord Nelson Inn, turn left (north-eastwards) and follow a road to reach the main A1133. Turn left, with care, and follow the main road towards Collingham. At the village of Langford, take the footpath on the left, going over a stile and across several grassy fields to reach Old Hall Farm. Here, walk northwards, passing the farm buildings and a farm shop. Cross another field to reach a road. Go straight over and follow the lane opposite, going through a gate beside Langford Church. Continue northwards along a track, heading towards the Nottingham to Lincoln railway line. Cross the railway, with care, at the level crossing and continue along the track.

This track leads to the boundary of a quarry. Here, the quarry company have established an alternative route to the right, following a track around the site, though it is possible to keep to the right of way through the quarry if you wish: the paths are reunited by a small wood on the far side of the quarry. Walk northwards beside the wood, then continue beside a ditch, keeping the tower of All Saints' Church in sight.

At the outskirts of **Collingham**, the path turns right, crossing the ditch, and then turns left into Little Lane. Follow Little Lane to reach Church Street from where it is a short step back to the start.

POINTS OF INTEREST:

Holme – This quaint village once was on the west bank of the River Trent. A great flood changed the course of the river and Holme then found itself on the east bank.
Collingham – This was originally a Saxon settlement that developed into North and South Collingham. A Saxon Cross still stands at the northern end of the village. The current combined village was amalgamated under one Parish Council in 1974.

REFRESHMENTS:
The Lord Nelson, Winthorpe.
There are several opportunities in Collingham.

Walk 84   THE RIVER IDLE $7^1/_2$m (12km)

Maps: OS Sheets Landranger 120; Pathfinder 745.

Man-made lakes that are now the habitat of wetland birds.

Start: At 691859, the telephone box on Daneshill Road, at the centre of Lound.

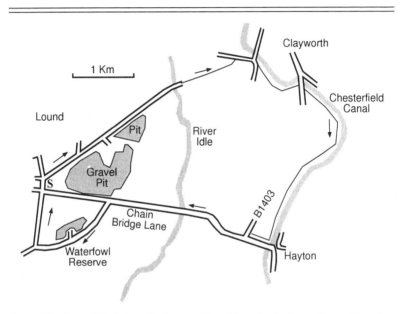

Car parking is possible in Lound: please park considerately. At the nearby road junction, turn left and walk along Town Street, passing the Bluebell Inn. Turn right along Neatholme Road, a public bridleway. Follow the unmade road to a metal barrier. Go past the barrier and continue north-eastwards, watching out for riders who use this section of the bridleway to exercise their horses.

As you continue along the lane you will see gravel pit lakes on the right and an open cast quarry on the left. On reaching a Y-junction, take the left-hand (straight ahead) alternative. You will now see lakes on both sides of the track. These lakes attract a wide variety of wildfowl, including migrants from other continents. Continue along the track to the River Idle.

Cross the river by the footbridge and maintain direction through trees, passing a low wooden barrier. Once through the woods, cross a dyke by way of another bridge and cross the arable field beyond towards the village of Clayworth. Cross another ditch and follow a farm track beside a hedge for 150 yards to reach a fence. Cross the fence, turn right along an unmade track and follow it to reach a bridge over the Chesterfield Canal.

Do not cross the bridge: instead, turn right to walk along the towpath on the canal's western bank, heading towards Hayton. On this section of the canal you will pass the moorings for the narrow boats belonging to the Retford and Worksop Boat Club. The canal meanders through delightful farmland on the edge of the River Idle valley: to the west you can see across the shallow valley to Lound and Sutton.

Leave the canal at the Boat Inn and turn right, with care, along the B1403. Follow the road westwards for 500 yards to reach a sharp right bend. Now leave the road, maintaining direction along the unmade Chain Bridge Lane. Follow the lane over the River Idle and continue towards Lound, with views of the area's sand pits which are still being worked. About 1,100 yards from the bridge over the Idle, turn left to follow another lane to Sutton Grange. This lane leads you to the **Wetlands Waterfowl Reserve**. Beyond the Reserve the lane reaches a road: turn right and follow the road back to the start.

POINTS OF INTEREST:
Wetlands Waterfowl Reserve – Set in 32 acres of lakes and woodland, Wetlands is home to over 100 different kinds of bird, chiefly waterfowl.

REFRESHMENTS:
The Bluebell Inn, Lound.
The Boat Inn, Hayton.

Walk 85　　　　NORMANTON　　　　$7\frac{1}{2}$m (12km)

Maps: OS Sheets Landranger 129; Pathfinder 853.

A walk along the River Soar.

Start: At 504233, the car park in Zouch.

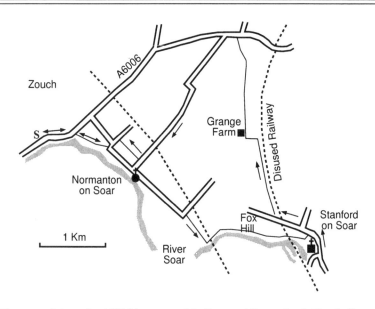

The car park is on the A6006 just west of the Rose and Crown Inn in Zouch. From it, walk eastwards along the A6006, crossing the River Soar. Now turn right by a farmyard, following footpath signs across a grassy field to a gate and across the grassy field beyond. Go over a stile into a third grassy field and cross this to reach a stile. Cross on to Main Street, Normanton on Soar. Turn right along Main Street, passing the Plough Inn with its picturesque riverside garden, to reach **St James' Church**. Turn right into the churchyard and walk to the church door. Opposite the church door, there is a stile in the tall, neat hedge: go over the stile and follow a footpath across a private garden to reach another stile. Go over into a field with a collection of wooden weekend retreats. Follow the footpath signs to a stile into a grassy field. Cross the field to reach a lonely stile surrounded by open grass. Cross a wooden bridge over a narrow ditch and go over the nearby stile to return to the road that was Main Street. Turn right and walk along the lane to a sharp bend. There, maintain direction along a footpath through a narrow field. Go over a stile into a grassy field and cross to reach the railway line to your left. Go over another stile and cross the line with great care - this is the main Intercity line linking Sheffield and Nottingham with London Euston. Cross yet another stile into fields on the bank of the River Soar.

Turn left (eastwards) along the river crossing stiles linking fields as the path rises above the riverbank to skirt a small woodland. Go over a fence on the left, where the wire is replaced by wooden slats, and cross the field beyond to reach another railway line, this one disused. Cross the line into a grassy field. Turn right and follow yellow arrows across four stiles, heading towards the church in Stanford on Soar. To the right, beyond the hawthorns is the River Soar. The path turns left and follows a fence into Stanford, reaching a road 50 yards north of St John the Baptist Church. Turn left and walk along the road towards Normanton. At the road junction, continue along the Normanton road, going up Fox Hill to where the road crosses the disused railway line. Now turn right along a signed footpath, climbing the bank into an arable field. Walk along the top of the west cutting of the disused railway, with excellent views across the surrounding farmland, to reach another bridge across the line. At this point the footpath becomes a bridleway. Continue northwards along the bridleway, which runs beside the disused railway. The bridleway turns left, leaving the railway line to follow a field boundary, then turns right to reach Grange Farm. Follow the blue bridleway signs past the farm, going gently uphill to reach the A6006.

Turn left, with care, along the A6006 and then, after 50 yards, go left again along a country lane to Normanton on Soar. The lane leads gently downhill, giving the walker excellent views across fields into Leicestershire. Follow the lane across the main railway and down into Normanton. At the 30 mph speed limit sign, turn right along a footpath, following it across three grassy meadows and then through an alley beside houses to reach Far Lane. Turn left and walk into Main Street, Normanton. At the sharp bend, cross a stile into a field and reverse the outward route back to the car park.

POINTS OF INTEREST:

St James Church, Normanton on Soar – The church was built in 1200AD. The tall broached spire is considered to be the best example in the country.

REFRESHMENTS:

The Rose and Crown, Zouch.
The Plough Inn, Normanton.

Walk 86   BARNBY IN THE WILLOWS   7¹/₂m (12km)

Maps: OS Sheets Landranger 121; Pathfinder 797.

A picturesque walk through Fenland.

Start: At 836546, the Plough Inn, Coddington.

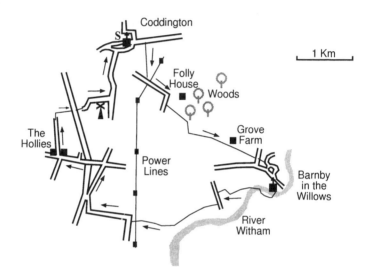

Please park carefully and with consideration in the village. Walk out of the village along the Sleaford Road, heading eastwards for 100 yards, then following a signed path on the right, beside 'The Bungalow'. Go over a stile into a grassy field and head southwards to reach another stile. Cross this and another grassy field to reach a third stile. Go over into an arable field. Walk along the right hedgerow to a farm track. Turn left along the track for 500 yards to reach a track junction just before Folly House. Follow the track for 150 yards to reach the first hedge on the left. Turn left and walk though a field, with the hedgerow on your right, aiming for the woods ahead. Go over a stile into the woods and follow a clear path south-eastwards. Now turn right and walk beside the wood to reach a ditch. There are many paths through the woods so you will need to check your position on emerging. You may need to turn left to reach the ditch, which has a wide bridge across it. Walk southwards across an arable field, with the ditch on your left, to reach a junction of ditches. Turn left beside the ditch and walk east-south-east towards Grove Farm.

The path enters the garden of Grove Farm and then crosses a bridge over the ditch on the right. Now follow the yellow footpath signs to the left, following the ditch to the corner of the field. Turn right and walk beside the hedge to reach a footpath sign. Turn left into another arable field and follow the hedge to a stile. Go over into a grassy field and cross it to reach a lane. Cross the lane and follow the signed footpath almost opposite, over a stile and into a paddock. Go through the paddock to reach Back Lane, Barnby in the Willows. Go along the lane, then turn right into Dark Lane, following it to **Front Street**. Turn left to reach All Saints' Church. Now follow the footpath through the churchyard to a reach bridge over the River Witham. Cross and turn right, walking westwards along the riverbank for 250 yards to reach a farm bridge. Cross to the northern bank of the river and follow the yellow footpath signs along hedges beside Shire Dyke. The path leaves the dyke to follow the hedgerow (north-north-west, then west-south-westwards) to reach a farm track. Turn left and walk down the track to rejoin Shire Dyke.

Now follow the footpath signs along the banks of Shire Dyke for $1^1/_4$ miles as it passes through arable fields towards Balderton and Newark. The path reaches a farm lane beneath power lines: turn right, then, after 50 yards, turn left into Fen Lane, following it west towards the A1. Near the A1, turn right along Coddington Road and follow it towards Coddington for 800 yards to reach a crossroads. Turn left (westwards) and walk along Barnby Road, crossing over the A1. At The Hollies turn right (northwards) up the track to 'The Firs'. Now turn right along Clay Lane, following it under the A1 to reach Coddington Lane by an old windmill. Turn left and follow the lane into Coddington to return to the start.

POINTS OF INTEREST:

Front Street, Barnby in the Willows – The old coach road from Newark to Sleaford passed through Barnby in the Willows, the coaches rumbling along Front Street then crossing the River Witham into Lincolnshire. The Willows in 'Barnby in the Willows' refers to the local willow osiers used for basket making in the last century.

REFRESHMENTS:

The Hungry Horse, Main Street, Coddington.
The Plough Inn, Main Street, Coddington.
The Willow Tree, Barnby in the Willows.

Walk 87   **STAUNTON IN THE VALE** $7^1/_2$m (12km)
Maps: OS Sheets Landranger 129 and 130; Pathfinder 813 and 814.

A walk offering excellent views across three counties.

Start: At 806436, the Staunton Arms, Staunton in the Vale.

If you use the inn car park, please check with the landlord beforehand. Walk southwards along the lane opposite the inn but, when it bends left to go to Staunton Hall, go over a stile to the right of a gate and walk along the green lane beyond. Go though a gate on the right, just before arriving at the church, and cross the grass field beyond to reach a bridge over a ditch. Cross the bridge and the grass field beyond to reach a gate close to a bend in a road. Go over a stile and walk along a path through a shrubbery to reach a private church. Go on to a lane and turn right to reach the road. Turn left and follow the road to a bridge across a disused railway.

The footpath from here to Flawborough has been diverted due to the open cast mining activities of British Gypsum, so continue along the road to reach the hamlet of Alverton. Turn right and walk along the road to Flawborough. The footpaths in Flawborough have been realigned and are not as shown on the Ordnance Survey maps. Take a path going westwards across an open field to cut off the corner of the road as it bends left by the church. When you regain the road, take the path opposite, walking along a line of trees to reach the River Devon.

Turn right along the riverbank to reach a brick farm bridge. Turn left, over the bridge, and follow the track beyond to a road. Turn right and follow the road through the quaint village of **Shelton**. The views from this road are magnificent. Follow the road as it bends left, north-westwards. then turn right at a road junction. Cross Wensor Bridge (over the River Devon) and continue along the road to reach Booth Farm. Continue along the road as it bends left (northwards) to reach a junction about 250 yards further on. Turn right along this high road with its magnificent views across Nottinghamshire, Lincolnshire and Leicestershire.

Follow the road to a T-junction and turn right. Now follow the road towards Staunton, but take time to explore the **Staunton Quarry Nature Reserve**. Two kilometres along the road, take a footpath on the right across arable fields to reach a farm track. Turn right and follow the track back to Staunton.

POINTS OF INTEREST:
Shelton – Set above the River Devon the views from the road passing through the village are excellent. On a good day you can see as far as Belvoir Castle, to the south, and St Mary's Church in Newark, to the north.
Staunton Quarry Nature Reserve – The Reserve is managed by the Nottinghamshire Wildlife Trust. Formerly a quarry, the Reserve is home to aquatic wildlife, from invertebrates through to ducks and geese.

REFRESHMENTS:
The Staunton Arms, Staunton in the Vale.

Walk 88 GUNTHORPE BRIDGE AND HAZELFORD FERRY 8m (13km)

Maps: OS Sheets Landranger 129; Pathfinder 813.

Past gravel pit lakes, returning along the River Trent.

Start: At 682437, the car park near Gunthorpe Bridge.

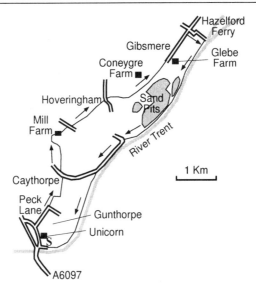

From the car park near the **Gunthorpe Bridge**, opposite the Unicorn Hotel, walk north-westwards through the village, following Main Street. Turn right along Peck Lane, following it into farmland behind Gunthorpe village. When the lane bends sharply to the right, go straight ahead, following a footpath between two fields. After 250 yards the path makes a right-angled turn to the right and follows a hedge (the hedge is on your left). After 200 yards the path turns equally sharply left and crosses a footbridge over a small stream. Continue along the footpath as it goes over two more footbridges and then enters the village of Caythorpe by way of the driveway of a private house. Cross another stream and go over a stile to reach Main Street immediately opposite the Black Horse Inn.

Turn left along Main Street for 200 yards, re-crossing the stream by a telephone box. Now turn right along a footpath, following it, beside a small stream that runs along the side a field, to reach Mill Farm. As you enter the farmyard you will see the remains of the old mill race. Signposts guide you straigthforwardly around the farm and on to a bridleway heading north-eastwards. Cross a minor road and continue north-eastwards to reach another minor road. Cross this and continue along the bridleway. On the right you may see sailing boats on a lake: the lake is a filled gravel pit, a remnant from the days when aggregates were excavated locally. The boats belong to the Nottinghamshire County Sailing Club (NCSC).

Follow the bridleway through Glebe Farm, keeping the farm buildings to your right, and continue to Gibsmere. Here, take the second turning on the right, by Gibsmere Farm. Follow this lane and, just after passing Manor House, turn left and cross a field to reach a Z-bend in a minor road. Follow this minor road to Hazelford Ferry, ignoring the footpaths as marked on the OS maps. The OS have yet to catch up with the realignment of these paths.

The route now follows the north bank of the River Trent back to Gunthorpe Bridge, this section of the walk forming part of the Trent Valley Way. The field gates along this section of the route are unique, each consisting of two gates, one on either side of the support post. As the walker passes through each gate it closes by gravity. On a sunny day along this section of the route the walker will meet all sorts of pleasure seekers: other walkers, anglers on the banks and folk in pleasure craft, all enjoying the river. Sailing boats on the NCSC lake can be seen to the right.

Follow the riverside path to reach a minor road. Go ahead along the road, but soon leave it, returning to the river and following it to reach the weir at Gunthorpe Lock, a honey-pot for tourists on a warm sunny weekend afternoon. Now continue along the lane to return to the start.

POINTS OF INTEREST:

Gunthorpe Bridge – This is the only bridge across the River Trent between Trent Bridge, Nottingham and Newark. The present bridge was opened in 1927. Previously there was a toll bridge, the old toll house, near the lock, now being a restaurant.

REFRESHMENTS:
The Unicorn Inn, Gunthorpe.
Tom Browns, Gunthorpe.
The Anchor Inn, Gunthorpe.
The Black Horse Inn, Caythorpe.
The Hazelford Ferry Inn, Boat Lane, Bleasby.

Walk 89   **KNEESALL AND MAPLEBECK**   8m (13km)
Maps: OS Landranger 120; Pathfinder 780.
Typical North Nottinghamshire farmland scenery.
Start: At 702643, in the village of Kneesall.

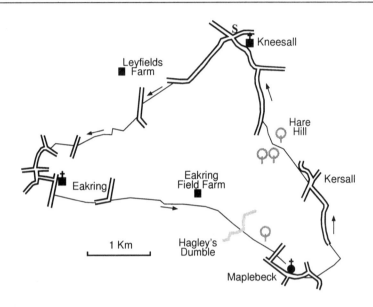

On-street parking is possible in Kneesall, but please park considerately. The walk
starts by the small triangular green: cross the A616, with care, to the bridleway opposite
and go down this wide, grassy track to reach a paddock. The gate has a padlocked
chain, so go over the fence beside it, cross the paddock and go over a stile. The track
now turns right: go along it for 200 yards to reach a signpost that points the way
across a field towards an obvious gap in a hedge. Cross the next field keeping the
small coppice on the horizon just to the left of your line of walking. As you continue,
the disused windmill in Eakring comes into view. When you reach a tarmac track,
turn left along it to where it bends left. Here, cross a concrete bridge into a field and
follow the hedge on the right to reach another field, differentiated more by use than
actual boundary. Follow the boundary to right to reach the track leading to Leyfields
Farm. Turn left and walk along the track for 150 yards, then turn right along a path.

Follow the path to reach a lane close to the disused windmill, now a private dwelling. Turn left and follow the lane into Eakring.

Turn left by the Savile Arms and then right into Church Lane. At the bend in the lane you can take a short diversion along a farm track to see **Mompesson Cross**. The route continues along Church Lane to reach the Kirklington road opposite St Andrew's Church. Turn right and walk to the Post Office and Stores. Opposite the Post Office, turn down Triumph Road to reach the playing fields. Now follow the footpath signs westwards across a ditch and into fields. Cross a stream (Hagley's Dumble) then follow the ubiquitous yellow arrows, crossing another field towards the centre of a coppice that is NOT shown on the OS Landranger map. As you climb towards the trees there are good views across The Beck to Kneesall. Walk along the side of the coppice and then across another field to reach a country lane.

Cross the lane and follow the path opposite, passing an equestrian training site before arriving at the church in Maplebeck. Turn right here to visit the Beehive Inn. The route turns left, following a lane out of the hamlet to reach a footpath on the right. Follow this across a field to reach another road. Turn right for 50 yards, then go left along a footpath, following it to a stream (The Beck). Cross a brick bridge and the field beyond to reach a hedge. Turn left and follow a path into Kersall. Walk through the hamlet and take a track heading north-westwards. When the track bends right, go straight on, along a footpath, following yellow signs as you cross fields to reach the woodland on Hare Hill. Turn right and follow the edge of the wood to reach a cinder track. Turn left and, still following the woodland edge, walk towards a hedge. Go through the hedge: there are good views of Kneesall from here. Continue along the path as it crosses the field ahead, aiming for the tower of St Bartholomew's Church. The path reaches a farm track: follow this to return to the village of Kneesall.

POINTS OF INTEREST:

Mompesson Cross – William Mompesson worked in Eyam between September 1665 and October 1666 during the Great Plague. Three years later he was appointed to the rectorship of Eakring. However the villagers were so afraid that he might still carry the disease that they made him live for a time in a hut in Rufford Park. The cross marks the spot where Mompesson would preach during his exile. Mompesson stayed at Eakring until his death in 1708.

REFRESHMENTS:
The Savile Arms, Eakring.
The Beehive Inn, Maplebeck.
The Angel Inn, Kneesall.

Walk 90   **BOTHAMSALL**   8m (13km)

Maps: OS Sheets Landranger 120; Pathfinder 763.
An unspoilt village and fine North Midland farmland.
Start: At 675734, Bothamsall Church.

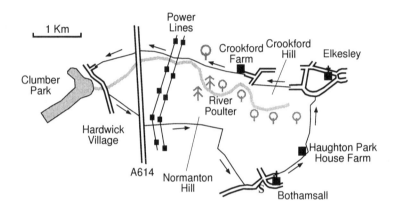

Leave Bothamsall along the lane beside the church, heading east-north-east. The track passes quaint ivy-covered cottages before becoming a farm track, and then a path, leading towards Haughton Park House Farm. At the farm, signs for the Robin Hood Way appear: follow these northwards around the farm, then cross a private road, with chestnut trees, and follow the bridleway opposite through fields to reach the delightful red-brick houses nestling beneath Elkesley Wood. The path passes in front of the cottages, the Robin Hood Way arrows guiding you through the wood beyond to reach a bridge crossing the River Poulter.

Cross the bridge and the field beyond to reach Brough Lane. Turn left and walk along the lane to Crookford Hill. Go past the conspicuously guarded Osbournes Mill, and continue to where the lane ends at a road junction. Turn right along the road for 150 yards, then turn left along a farm track/bridleway to reach Crookford Farm. Follow the bridleway through the farm and across fields to reach a patch of woodland. Go through the woodland, emerging into a field on the other side. The River Poulter is close by on your left as you continue along the bridleway to reach the A614.

Cross the A614, with care, and take the footpath immediately opposite, following it through woods and then across a field to reach a road. Turn left and follow the road into **Hardwick Village**. Walk through this charming village to reach a T-junction. Turn left and walk along the road to reach a ford through the River Poulter. There is a footbridge for pedestrians. Beyond the river, turn into the second field on the left and follow a well-used bridleway across it to reach Cabin Hill Covert. Go through a gate and walk along the road beyond for a few yards to reach the A614. Turn right and walk beside the main road as far as the next road into Clumber Park.

Here, cross the A614, again with care, and go eastwards along a bridleway, following the signs for the Robin Hood Way through woodland. The bridleway leaves the woods, becoming a track between fields. Turn right at another bridleway sign and walk along a track for 400 yards to reach a group of dilapidated barns.

Turn left and follow a path towards the village of Bothamsall. The path follows hedges, and then crosses an arable field to reach a clump of trees. The trees are on a mound beside a road: turn left along the road to return to Bothamsall.

POINTS OF INTEREST:
Hardwick Village – This beautiful unspoilt village lies deep in Clumber Park. Both the post and telephone boxes are painted green.

REFRESHMENTS:
There are no places for refreshment along this route, the nearest being at Walesby to the south.

Walk 91   CALVERTON $8^1/_2$m (14km)

Maps: OS Sheets Landranger 120 and 129; Pathfinder 795, 796, 812 and 813.

A long walk, but one with magnificent views.

Start: At 629515, the Oxton Village Hall car park.

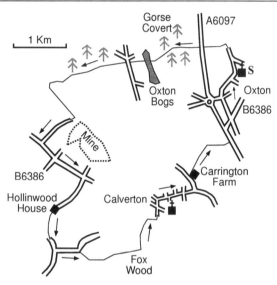

Turn left along Main Street passing the Post Office. Continue northwards along Forest Road for 150 yards, then turn left along a signed bridleway. Follow the bridleway through a farmyard and a field to reach a large lay-by on the A6097 dual carriageway. Cross this busy trunk road with care: the central reservation, with its silver birches, offers you the chance to take stock before completing the crossing. Go through a wooden kissing gate into the Oxton Estate. Cross the grassy field to reach a stile into Gorse Covert, a coniferous woodland. Follow a well-marked path through the wood and across a field (walking beside a stream) to reach a farm track. Now follow yellow signs across the track and into scrubland called Oxton Bogs. The ponds are well hidden from the walker by the scrub, although the wildfowl will be heard. Cross an arable field to reach Wimbush Lane at its junction with another road. Cross the roads and follow a footpath westwards.

172

The path crosses a railway line serving the Calverton mine, then ascends through an arable field. Follow the path between a colliery spoil heap, on the right, and a coniferous woodland, on the left. Yellow footpath signs now direct you along a track through the forest. The track makes an S bend, first left and then right: at the right bend, follow a path along a line of telegraph poles beside the boundary to the colliery. Continue to follow the telegraph poles when they leave the forest, the path descending beside an arable field from where there is a good view of the winding towers at Calverton Colliery. When the path reaches a track, turn right and follow the track to a lane. Turn left and follow the lane to the B6386. Cross and continue along the lane opposite. At Hollinwood Lane, turn right and walk uphill along the track to Hollinwood House. On either side of the track is Ramsdale Golf Course. Go to the right of Hollinwood House and continue uphill, going through the golf course to reach a coppice. The path curves left around the coppice giving magnificent views to the north and east. Go over a stile on to a cinder track and follow the track southwards as it becomes a drive and leads to a lane (George's Lane), reaching it at a sharp bend.

Walk eastwards along the wide grass verge of George's Lane. After 400 yards the road makes another sharp bend: continue straight ahead along a bridleway. The bridleway goes along the crest of a ridge and gives yet more magnificent views – to the north across fields to Calverton and beyond, and to the south-east to Woodborough. The track becomes a green lane bounded by hedges as it descends to Fox Wood. At Fox Wood, take the signed footpath on the left, crossing an arable field and going around a coppice to reach the outskirts of Calverton. Now take a path on the right, following it through Renals Way to reach the centre of the village. Cross the Market Square and take the path behind the shops to reach Crookdole Lane. Turn right and walk to a crossroads. Cross and continue along Crookdole Lane to reach Carrington Lane. Turn left and walk along the track to reach a signed footpath at Carrington Farm. Turn right and follow the yellow arrows across fields to reach Dover Beck, continuing to reach the A6097.

Cross, with care, turn left and walk beside the road for 200 yards to reach a farm track opposite Mill Farm. Turn right and follow the track for 200 yards to reach the B6386. Turn left and walk through the picturesque village of Oxton to return to the start.

REFRESHMENTS:
The Green Dragon, Blind Lane, Oxton.
Ye Olde Bridge Inn, Nottingham Road, Oxton.
There are also many opportunities in Calverton.

Walk 92   **EAST LEAKE**   9m (16km)

Maps: OS Sheets Landranger 129; Pathfinder 853.

A walk through fine south Nottinghamshire scenery.

Start: At 555265, the Library/Leisure Centre car park, East Leake.

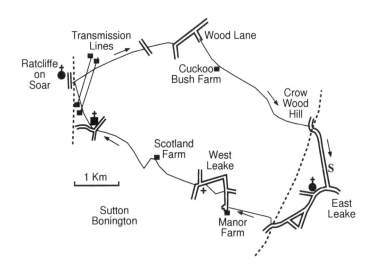

The car park is next to the Fire Station in Gotham Lane. From it, turn left (southwards) and walk into the town. On reaching Main Street, turn right, passing the Catholic Church and continuing to the Parish Church of St Mary, near the Green. A river, Sheepwash Brook, runs through the Green. Main Street becomes Brook Side: continue along it to reach a Y-junction. Now follow Woodgate Road, signed for Hathern Station and Ashby, soon crossing a bridge over an old railway line. Just beyond the bridge, turn right along a signed footpath to West Leake. From this clearly defined path there are excellent views of the Ratcliffe-on-Soar Power Station. Go into the farmyard of Manor Farm, and turn right to follow a track towards West Leake. The track soon meets a minor road: here, make a sharp left turn and follow a path that runs parallel with Kingston Brook. After 250 yards, go through a gate and immediately turn sharp right to cross a small bridge over Kingston Brook. Bear left across the field beyond to

174

reach steps, and a handrail, into the churchyard of **West Leake**. Go through the churchyard to reach a road and turn left. At a bend in the road, go straight on along a track to Scotland Farm. Keep on the track. Turn sharp left on entering the farmyard, passing a dew pond and heading south-westwards towards Sutton Bonnington. When you reach Kingston Brook, turn right and follow a path along its northern bank. After 250 yards the path reaches a bridge over the Brook: cross and turn right to continue along the southern side of the Brook.

Nearing **Kingston on Soar** the walker is treated to a magnificent view of Kingston Hall. Go over a stile 100 yards south of Kingston Brook and turn right to follow a road to the village green, opposite the church. Nearby are an old water pump, and an old red telephone kiosk: take the path beside the telephone box, heading northwards between houses, crossing Kingston Brook again to reach a field. Follow the obvious path across the field, heading towards a railway embankment and passing under the power lines coming from the Ratcliffe power station. On reaching the railway the walker may pass under the railway to visit the tiny village of Ratcliffe-on-Soar, though there is little there except a church. From the embankment turn right along an obvious path heading north-west across a field and then through a small coppice. The next section of the route has been affected by work for the power station and so the footpath has been redirected. Careful navigation is needed in places to keep to the new route, though as time and feet pass, the new path will become more clearly defined. Cross a lane and continue along a now obvious path. After 500 yards, at a Y-junction, take the right fork to reach, after a further 200 yards, another minor road. Turn left along the road for 500 yards, then turn right along Wood Lane, following it to Cuckoo Bush Farm. Continue along a clear path over Court Hill to Crow Wood Hill, passing the clubhouse of Rushcliffe Golf Course and Rushcliffe Nursing Home, to reach a lane where it crosses a railway line. Follow the lane back into East Leake, the lane taking you directly back to the car park.

POINTS OF INTEREST:

West Leake – The 12th-century church has neither a spire nor a tower, but it does have twin bells in a small assembly over the nave. There is also a pair of sundials. The lych-gate commemorates those who fell in the 1914-18 War.

Kingston on Soar – The old cast iron pump was once the village's sole water supply.

REFRESHMENTS:

None on the route, but there is a good choice in East Leake.

Walk 93   THE SOUTHWELL TRAIL   9m (14km)

Maps: OS Landranger 120; Pathfinder 796.

This walk follows a former railway line, now a linear park.

Start: At 706544, the Southwell Trail Car Park, Station Road, Southwell.

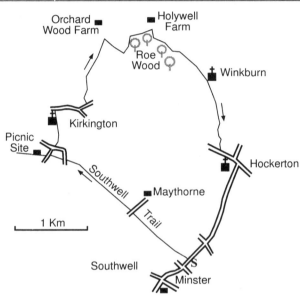

Leave the car park along the Trail, a cinder track which was formerly a railway, closed when Dr Beeching became the head of British Rail. The Trail heads north-westwards, passing the backs of houses on the outskirts of Southwell. After about a mile, the Trail crosses a lane leading to Maythorne, then maintains direction into the country, delightful views of which are seen through the hedgerows. The Trail now curves left and goes under two bridges to reach the Kirklington car park and picnic site. Here, leave the Trail, passing a former railway building, now a private house, to reach a road. Turn left and walk along the road to reach a T-junction. Turn right, and, after 25 yards, left along a footpath marked with a Robin Hood Way sign, passing Osmanthorpe Manor. The path crosses a tributary of the River Greet by way of a concrete bridge, then passes a pond that is NOT marked on the OS Landranger map.

Cross another tributary of the River Greet, then follow the path signs to reach Church Farm. Continue along the farm track to reach the A617 in the village of Kirklington, opposite Rodney School.

Turn right and walk along the A617, with care, for 300 yards, then turn left along a bridleway, passing Rodney School and then climbing through parkland, with good views towards Farnsfield. The bridleway emerges on to a plateau: follow the signs for the Robin Hood Way across the high farmland, heading towards two barns. Beyond the barns the path follows a line of power lines on wooden poles between two fields and beside a ditch. Where the ditch makes a left turn, cross it by way of a wooden bridge and walk into a coppice. Follow the path through the coppice to meet another path. Turn right, still following the Robin Hood Way signs, and walk through the coppice as it forms the boundary between two fields. When the path emerges from the coppice, go left to walk around the northern side of Roe Wood. Follow the edge of the wood, with good views of the surrounding farmland (Orchard Wood Farm and Holywell Farm). Keeping Roe Wood on your right, continue along the path as it becomes a track (Roewood Lane) leading to the hamlet of Winkburn.

Cross the small green with its chestnut trees, then follow a path through a hedge, crossing a rickety stile. Cross the meadow beyond, which is set out for equestrian events and continue to reach the end of a farm track. Now cross a field to its opposite, south-eastern, corner, go through the hedge, and turn left to walk beside the hedge. Go through another hedge, leading off to the right, and continue along the top of the next field. Turn right at a hedge and walk down towards the A617. Just before arriving at a building there is a stile in the hedge on the right: cross this and follow the obvious footpath beyond to reach the main road. Turn left and, with care, follow the road into Hockerton. In the village, turn right and follow a country lane back to Southwell. After about a mile the towers of **Southwell Minster** will come into view: a further 800 yards of walking will now bring you back to the car park from which the walk started.

POINTS OF INTEREST:
Southwell Minster – There has been a church here since Saxon times. Southwell was made a bishopric in 1884. The Minster has many exquisite architectural features and is well worth the time spent visiting. The Minster is also famous for its school and choir.

REFRESHMENTS:
The Newcastle Arms, Southwell.
The Spread Eagle, Hockerton.

Walk 94　　　GRINGLEY ON THE HILL　　　9m (14km)

Maps: OS Sheets Landranger 112; Pathfinder 728 and 745.
A walk through picturesque farmland with magnificent views.
Start: At 744907, a lay-by on the A631.

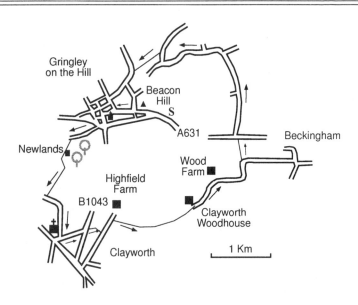

Walk westwards along the lane into Gringley on the Hill. At the crossroads by the beacon, turn right through a white kissing gate and climb **Beacon Hill** to enjoy the magnificent view. Return to the crossroads and continue westwards along High Street, passing the Blue Bell Inn and the Church of St Peter and St Paul. Follow the road as it bends south, then back west. At this second bend, cross the green to reach the A631. Cross the dual carriageway, with great care, to reach a footpath sign by a hedge. Use steps to cross a ditch into an arable field and cross the field south-westwards to reach a farm track. Turn right along the track, with magnificent views into North Nottinghamshire, until it disappears into another arable field. Maintain direction across the field to reach a hedge corner. Step through a large gap in the hedge into another arable field and cross to the hedgerow on the far side. Go through the hedge into the next field and turn left to walk with the hedgerow on your left. Keep to the side of the field as the hedgerow bends right to reach a coppice surrounding Newlands. Walk along the north-western edge of the wood, and, at its end, turn left along a path leading to the track for Newlands. Follow the track to the village of Clayworth, coming out on to Church Lane, between St Peter's Church and the cemetery.

Turn left along Church Lane to reach the B1403. Cross the road and follow the green lane opposite to a stile. Go over into a grassy field and walk along the right edge to reach another green lane. Turn left and follow the lane to its end by Highfield Farm. Go through a wooden gate and turn right into a grassy field. Walk along the field's left edge, soon reaching another green lane. Follow the lane to a gate. Go through and continue eastwards along the field edges, crossing a farm track and an arable field to reach a cross-paths. Continue eastwards across an arable field to reach Clayworth Woodhouse, the path offering excellent views, to the west, across farmland to the gravel lakes at Lound. Follow yellow footpath signs around the farm buildings to reach Wood Lane and follow the lane east towards Beckingham, passing Wood Farm. The lane bends left, then after 400 yards, back right. At this second bend, turn left (northwards) along a signed footpath across an arable field. At the top of the hill there is an excellent view across the surrounding countryside. Cross a wooden footbridge into another arable field and cross the field to reach a narrow ditch and a hedge leading to the A631.

Cross the A631, with care, to reach a track (West Road) opposite. Walk northwards along the track, with excellent views across the fenland into South Yorkshire. The track becomes metalled and changes name to Oaks Lane: continue along it to reach a road. Turn left and walk along the road to reach the top of Wooden Beck Hill and more good views. Continue to a road junction and turn right on to the B1403, following it to Lowfield Farm. Turn left and walk beside a ditch, following a line of telegraph poles. Keep to the edge of the field by turning left and walking 100 yards up to a hedgerow. Turn right and follow the hedge to Shaw Road. Walk uphill along the road, into Gringley on the Hill. By the playing fields Shaw Lane becomes Finkell Street: continue for 250 yards, then turn left along a footpath, crossing paddocks to reach High Street. Turn left to return to Beacon Hill and the start of the walk.

POINTS OF INTEREST:

Beacon Hill – Although only 82 metres (269 feet) above sea level, this view point offers expansive views northwards across fenland into South Yorkshire and eastwards to Lincoln Cathedral, while to the south, north Nottinghamshire is laid out.

REFRESHMENTS:
The Blue Bell Inn, Gringley on the Hill.

Walk 95   **THE DEVON VALLEY**   9m (15km)

Maps: OS Sheets Landranger 129; Pathfinder 813.

Through picturesque North Midland farming villages.

Start: At 759479, All Saints Church, Elston.

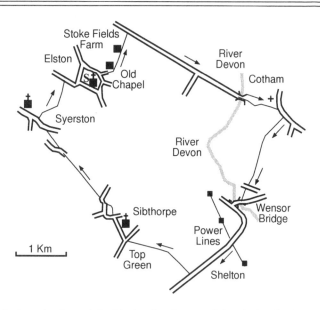

Go north along the footpath beside the church, around the playing field and take the path at the far end to reach Low Street. Turn left, and then right into Old Chapel Lane. At the end of the lane, go through a kissing gate into a grassy field to reach **Old Elston Chapel**. Cross the field and go through another kissing gate. Turn left and walk through the field, passing a commemorative Chestnut Tree. Go though Stoke Fields Farm yard and follow the farm drive to Moor Lane. Turn right and follow the lane for about $1^1/_4$ miles to where it makes a sharp right turn. Here, maintain direction (south-eastwards) along a bridleway, passing through fields. Cross the River Devon by a narrow brick bridge, looking out for the morbid inscription on top of one of the parapets – 'Alec died 17 September'. No year is given. The bridleway now becomes a narrow green lane with a dyke on its left side: cross the dyke at a bridge with a metal gate and continue along the green lane, ascending through grassy fields towards

Cotham. Go through a farm gate and turn left to visit old St Michael's Church. The church is in the care of the Church Conservation Trust. Note the wooden bell tower.

Now walk southwards along the road through Cotham, passing the smaller, brick-built St Michael's Church. Turn right along The Lane (a signed footpath), following it as it bends first left, then right. Now follows signs through the pretty gardens of the terraced cottages of The Row, then through a narrow alley between hedges to reach a stile. Cross and head south-westwards across a grassy field, aiming for an end-on hedge. Follow the hedge, then cross an arable field to reach a bridge across Back Dyke. Cross, turn left and walk along an embankment for 300 yards to where the dyke starts to bend right. Now cross the arable field, heading south-south-westwards at one of the pylons on the far horizon. Cross a farm track and then another arable field to reach a road at Wensor Bridge. Turn right and cross the bridge to reach a T-junction. Turn left and follow the lane into the tiny village of Shelton. From the lane there are excellent views to the right across the River Devon into the Vale of Belvoir as far as Belvoir Castle. Walk through Shelton with its ivy-covered cottages and squat church, then, just as you are leaving the village, turn right to cross a rickety bridge through a hedge into an arable field. Walk along the field edge, with a hedge on your right, then, when the hedge stops, maintain direction across the arable field. Cross a wooden bridge over an overgrown ditch and another field to reach a concrete bridge across a dyke. Cross and continue across open fields. The path becomes a farm track: continue along it to reach the hamlet of Top Green.

Follow the road to Sibthorpe, which has a stone dovecote and a church surrounded by a yew hedge, then go north-westwards on a path through Manor Farm to reach a Z-bend in Deadwong Lane. Walk from one bend to the next, then follow a signed path across two arable fields to reach a farm track. Go through a hedge and cross further arable fields to reach another track. Turn left and follow the track into Syerston, passing a brick pinfold. Now go over a signed stile and follow a narrow path beside a nursery to reach an arable field. Follow the yellow arrows along the field edge for 75 yards to reach a signpost. Cross the field to a group of trees, then follow the hedgerow on the left, and then the right, in the next field to reach Lodge Lane. Turn right and follow the lane back to Elston.

POINTS OF INTEREST:

Old Elston Chapel – The chapel has a Norman doorway. It is now maintained by the Redundant Churches Fund.

REFRESHMENTS:

The Chequers Inn, Toad Lane, Elston.

Walk 96   RANBY AND WORKSOP   9¹/₂m (15km)

Maps: OS Sheets Landranger 120; Pathfinder 744, 745, 762 and 763.

Along the Chesterfield Canal through picturesque farmland.

Start: At 649814, on the side of the lane, north of Ranby.

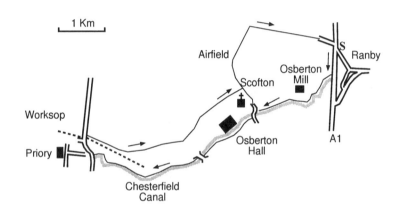

Walk southwards into Ranby to reach Bridge No. 51 over the Chesterfield Canal. Maintain direction along the towpath on the canal's west bank. Across the canal are the pretty gardens of the Ranby houses and a picnic area at the Chequers Inn, while to your right you can see the traffic on the A1. The canal curves right, around a field, and then goes under the A1 into open countryside. The noise of the road soon diminishes and you have a good view of Osberton Mill. Go under Bridge No. 50: there are now good views of Scofton Church. Osberton Lock is at Bridge No. 49: go under the bridge and then cross the canal by way of the lock gates, and continue along the towpath on the far side, heading towards Worksop. The path goes through the parkland of Osberton Hall, which is itself close to the opposite bank. By the Hall you go under a further two bridges. At the third bridge after Osberton Lock, recross the canal and continue into Worksop along the opposite bank, passing beneath a railway line on the way.

As you approach Worksop the scenery becomes gradually more industrial to the south, while to the north, beyond the fields, there are houses. On the outskirts of Worksop the canal bends sharp right and, later, sharp left as an aqueduct carries it across the River Ryton. Go under a road to reach another lock (the third on the walk). Cross the lock and continue along the towpath into the town centre. At the next road (Bridge No. 43) leave the canal by going under the bridge and then turning left. When you reach the road you must turn right if you wish to visit **Worksop Priory**, retracing your steps to this point to continue the walk. The walk follows Kilton Road to reach a mini-roundabout. Cross Kilton Hill and continue along Kilton Road, which now passes through a housing estate. Go under the railway and turn immediately right to follow an un-named road beside the railway for 250 yards. Now veer left, away from the railway, going through fields towards Scofton. The track rises to a trig. point by the entrance to a sewerage works. From the trig. point there are good views across the canal to Worksop.

Continues along the (now unmade) track to reach a cross-tracks. Maintain direction: soon you will be able to see Osberton Hall across its parkland. Scofton Church can also be seen. At a T-junction of tracks you have a choice of routes. Go right to see the church and then continue to the canal and follow it back to Ranby, or go left, heading north-west through parkland to reach a disused airfield. Cross the airfield and take the metalled track on the right, heading north-east. About 650 yards along this track you will reach a junction with bridleway signs: turn right and follow the bridleway to the A1. In favourable conditions, and with great care, you can cross the dual carriageway, but it is much more prudent to turn right and walk along the grassy verge of the A1 for 650 yards to reach the canal and then to turn left to follow the towpath back to the start.

POINTS OF INTEREST:

Worksop Priory – All that now remains of the priory is the lovely 14th-century gatehouse which has three arches that are still in splendid condition. Adorned with gables and buttresses, and saints in canopied niches the gatehouse was also a guest house. Beside the priory is the twin-towered Church of St Mary and St Cuthbert.

REFRESHMENTS:

The Chequers Inn, Ranby.

There are many opportunities in Worksop.

Walk 97   CLARBOROUGH AND NORTH LEVERTON   9³/₄m (15km)

Maps: OS Sheets Landranger 120; Pathfinder 745.

Green lanes across high North Midlands farmland.

Start: At 734832, St John the Baptist's Church, Clarborough.

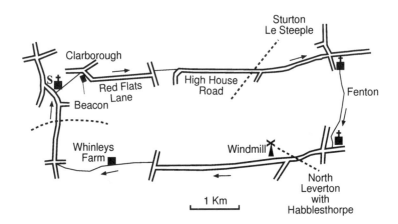

Take the footpath between the church and the Old Vicarage, passing a school and continuing along a short green lane. At the top of the lane, go over the stile on the left and head diagonally across the narrow grassy field beyond. Go through a gate and follow a hedge uphill to reach a beacon and a junction of green lanes. From here there are excellent views of Lincolnshire, South Yorkshire and north Nottinghamshire. Take the lane on the right (Red Flats Lane) towards Sturton le Steeple: West Burton Power Station dominates the view from this lane.

Follow the lane to a T-junction. Turn left along Blue Stocking Lane and, after 50 yards, go right through a gate, following a sign for the Trent Valley Way. Follow the path along field edges to reach High House Road, a bridleway, at a sharp bend. Continue eastwards along this bridleway. You are still on the Trent Valley Way, and the cooling towers of the West Burton Power Station loom ever larger as you continue. Go through a tunnel under the Retford to Lincoln railway line and then along Springs Lane, following the lane into the village of Sturton le Steeple.

The lane ends at a crossroads: go straight across into Church Street and follow it between the Reindeer Inn and the Church. By the inn there is a beautiful pond, complete with ducks, and garden. Continue along Church Street until, after 400 yards it becomes Little Holland. Now turn right along a footpath, following the left edge of several grassy fields to Three Leys Lane near the hamlet of Fenton. Cross the lane and follow the waymarkers around Stone Cottage and across fields to the village of North Leverton with Habblesthorpe. The path crosses a stream and goes between houses to reach a road (Main Street). Turn right into the village, passing the Royal Oak Inn.

At the crossroads, go straight over, heading westwards along the road towards East Retford. Go under a railway bridge and then, at a bend in the road, bear right along Mill Lane, following it to **North Leverton Mill**. Walk past the mill and continue westwards along the green lane (now called Retford Gate), following it to reach a T-junction. Turn right (northwards) for 100 yards, then go left along a footpath which follows the northern edge of woodland to reach Whinleys Farm. Go through the farmyard and follow the path across fields to reach a wind pump. The path now descends across more fields to reach a crossing of green lanes. Take the lane leading northwards, following it back to Clarborough and the start of the walk.

POINTS OF INTEREST:
North Leverton Mill – This is one of only two working mills left in Nottinghamshire. It is owned and run by local people and is supported by English Heritage. It is open to visitors during the summer.

REFRESHMENTS:
The Reindeer Inn, Sturton le Steeple.
The Royal Oak, North Leverton.

Walk 98   KEYWORTH WOLDS   10m (16km)

Maps: OS Sheets Landranger 129; Pathfinder 834 and 854.
Through beautiful East Midlands scenery.
Start: At 614308, St Mary Magdalene Church, Keyworth.

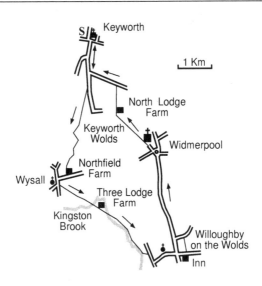

Car parking is available at the village hall in Elm Avenue. Leave the church southwards along Main Street, heading towards Wysall and Wymeswold. At the sharp right turn, continue southwards along Ling's Lane, an unmade lane with some houses on the left and fields beyond a hedge on the right. Just before reaching a Y-junction go over a signed stile on the right into a field, by a small pound. Turn left and follow a footpath through several fields, gently descending towards Fairham Brook. Near the brook the path crosses a field and enters a meadow sparsely populated with hawthorn trees. Cross a wooden bridge over the brook and continue through several arable fields, ascending towards Wysall. Crossing one field you will reach a hedge: turn left and walk along the hedge to reach a green lane. Turn right along the lane for 250 yards to reach a signed footpath on the left. Now follow the yellow signs across two fields and beside another. Go over a wooden fence in a barbed wire fence on the right and cross a paddock to reach Northfield Farm. Go through the farmyard to reach a road, and turn right into Wysall. At the T-junction, turn right to visit the Plough Inn. The route goes left along Main Street to Holy Trinity Church. Opposite the church, go down a signed path sign along a jitty beside the Village Hall into a children's play area. Cross to a stile and follow yellow arrows over stiles and fields to reach Kingston Brook. Cross the brook by stiles and bridge and go left to follow a field edge through several changes of direction. Follow yellow arrows between Thorpe Lodge Farm and a large wood, then go uphill aross a field (if the field has been ploughed aim for a telegraph pole), cross a stile and follow the left edge of the field beyond for 5 yards to reach a bridge. Recross Kingston Brook and turn right along a field edge to reach a lane. Cross the lane and several meadows following the yellow arrows. Cross a road to another path, following it through meadows to reach Willoughby-on-the-Wolds Church. Turn right down Church Lane, then turn left along Main Street.

At the crossroads, go straight over, then, opposite the Three Horseshoes Inn, take the footpath on the left, crossing meadows to reach a farm track. Turn left along the track to reach Widmerpool Road. Turn right along the road. The views from here are extensive, and include **Widmerpool Hall**. On reaching the village of Widmerpool, cross Wysall Road into Church Lane and follow it to its end. Now take the footpath on the left, following it to Fairham Brook. Cross the brook and walk along a drive to reach the **Church of St Peter and St Paul**. After a visit, continue along the drive to reach a footpath over a stile on the left. Take this, walking beside a field. Now, when the boundary to the woods on the right goes sharp right, maintain direction across the arable field, heading towards North Lodge Farm. Follow a farm track beside a field and around the farm buildings, and then go northwards across Keyworth Wolds to reach Wolds Lane. Turn left and follow Wolds Lane to Ling's Lane. Now turn right and reverse the outward route back to the start.

POINTS OF INTEREST:

Widmerpool Hall – Built in 1873, the Hall was formerly the home of Major Robertson. It is now the national training centre for the AA.

The Church of St Peter and St Paul, Widmerpool – The church has a 14th-century tower hung with bells dated 1592, 1609 and 1612.

REFRESHMENTS:

The Plough Inn, Selby Road, Keyworth.
The Salutation Inn, Main Street, Keyworth.
The Plough Inn, Keyworth Road, Wysall.
The Tress Horseshoes Inn, Willoughby-on-the-Wolds.

Walk 99   COLSTON BASSETT   10¹/₂m (17km)

Maps: OS Sheets Landranger 129; Pathfinder 834.

*A walk through typical East Midlands farmland and along a
section of the Grantham canal.*

Start: At 672369, the Foss Bridge Picnic Site car park.

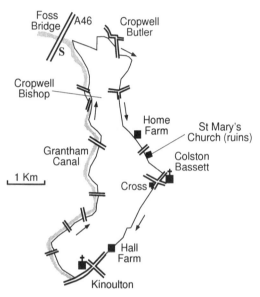

The Foss Bridge Picnic Site lies on the A46, Foss Way. Avoiding the site, take the
bridleway eastwards towards Cropwell Butler. The bridleway is very straight and
passes a coppice with a pond on the right. After about 1,000 yards, at a T-junction of
tracks, turn left, then, after about 400 yards, turn sharp right and follow How Lane
into Cropwell Butler. Cross into The Posts and follow this jitty to Main Street, reaching
it close to the Plough Inn. Turn right and follow Main Street to the corner with Tythby
Road. There, take the footpath heading south-westwards, passing allotments and then
crossing a field. Now go along a well-used track to reach a road. Cross the road, go
through a hedge and maintain direction along another well-used footpath. The path is

waymarked with yellow arrows on the fences and gateposts as it crosses several fields. As you approach Cropwell Bishop the distinctive tower of St Giles' Church provides a navigation aid. This section of the walk is part of a Grantham Canal Circular Walk.

Follow the path to reach a road, just a couple of yards to the right of Manor Farm. Go to the left of the farm buildings and follow a track for 1,000 yards. At the track's end, bear left and continue uphill to reach Home Farm. Go along the farm track, heading towards the spire of Colston Bassett church. When you reach a road, cross and follow the track opposite, passing the ruins of **St Mary's Church**. Go through a gate and walk around a cricket pitch to reach the village of Colston Bassett, crossing the infant River Smite before following a twitchel between some houses. Turn right into the village, passing the Church of St John the Divine. In the centre of the village is the **Village Cross.** Here, too, are the quaint village Post Office and General Store, and the Martins Arms Inn. Continue along School Lane: this becomes a bridleway and then a footpath. Cross the River Smite again, and follow well-marked footpaths along the edge of several fields to reach Hall Farm. Continue along the track into Kinoulton. Cross the village green and walk along Main Street, passing the Neville Arms Inn. Just beyond the Georgian St Luke's Church you will reach the **Grantham Canal**. Turn right and follow the towpath back to the Foss Picnic Site, a pleasant walk of about 5 miles. Approaching Cropwell Bishop the canal becomes a dry ditch, but British Waterways still maintain the path.

POINTS OF INTEREST:

St Mary's Church, Colston Bassett – The ruin is all that remains of this 13th- and 14th-century church, though the scaffolding suggests some restoration work is in progress. The graveyard is still in use with recent and well-tended grave stones.

Village Cross, Colston Bassett – Dating back to medieval times, the Cross was restored in 1831 and is now one of only two properties in Nottinghamshire owned by the National Trust.

Grantham Canal – Swans, coots, moorhens and various species of ducks populate the canal. The canal is no longer navigable, but the British Waterways Board maintains the towpath. At the Picnic Site you can see the detailed construction of the old, and now disused, lock gates.

REFRESHMENTS:

The Plough Inn, Cropwell Butler.
The Martins Arms Inn, Colston Bassett.
The Neville Arms Inn, Kinoulton.
There are also possibilities in Cropwell Bishop.

Walk 100   THE WELBECK ESTATE   14m (22km)

Maps: OS Sheets Landranger 120; Pathfinder 762.

A walk around one of the famous Dukeries estates.

Start: At 538744, the Creswell Crags Visitor Centre.

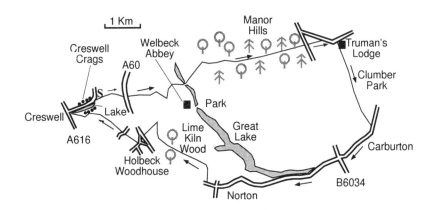

Leave the Visitor Centre along the Robin Hood Way, signs directing you past picnic tables and along a lane to reach the A60. Cross the road, with care, and continue along the metalled lane opposite, following bridleway signs eastwards to reach a concrete track. Follow this away from some farm buildings to reach the edge of woodland. Turn left and follow the woodland edge northwards. The woodland on your right gives way to playing fields, across which the walker will be able to see the castellated spires of Welbeck Abbey. When the bridleway meets a metalled track, turn right and follow the track for 100 yards into deciduous woodland. Now turn left and follow the Robin Hood Way for a further 50 yards. Turn left again, following the Robin Hood Way between a small lake, to the left, and the Great Lake to the right. Go through a fence and follow a broad track across fields and uphill to the woods on the Manor Hills. Follow the signed footpath through the woods to reach the lodges 50 yards away. At the lodges, turn right along a path into the woods. The path ascends through a sandstone gorge and then continues through the woodland, passing a disused lodge, white gates on both sides, and another lodge. On this stretch of the walk, beautiful deciduous woodland, is almost 2 miles long. Finally you reach the B6034.

Cross the road and continue along the bridleway opposite for 550 yards to reach a road. Turn right and follow the road to Truman's Lodge. Go through the arch of the Gatehouse into Clumber Park. Take the first avenue on the right (100 yards beyond the gatehouse). Go over a wooden barrier and follow the pleasant lane beyond to Carburton Bridge. Turn right and follow the road through Carburton to reach the B6034. Cross the road by the Olde School Tea Room and follow the road opposite. This road runs beside the Great Lake and passes a memorial to Lord George Bentinck.

At the quaint village of Norton, go straight ahead along a narrow lane for 500 yards, then turn right (northwards) along a signed path (Robin Hood Way). Go through a metal kissing gate to reach a road leading into the Welbeck Estate. Turn left (still on the Robin Hood Way) and follow the road through the estate. On the right you may see the deer that are raised on the estate. Go through Tile Kiln Wood to reach an inverted Y-junction. Go right to continue through the woods. At the next junction, turn left along an avenue of chestnut trees to reach the A60 at Woodhouse Hall.

Cross the road, with care, and go along the lane opposite, towards Holbeck Woodhouse, to reach a junction. Here, take the signed lane to the right. Follow this tree-lined lane past a cemetery, on the left, and into the village of Holbeck, reaching it opposite Woodside Cottage. Turn left, then after a few yards, at the telephone box and a seat for the weary, turn right to follow a footpath past some pretty cottage gardens to reach a green lane. Continue for 50 yards, then cross a stile into a grassy field. To the right there are good views into the Welbeck Estate. Cross stiles and fields to reach the top of **Creswell Crags**. From here the village of Creswell is laid out below you. Now follow the Robin Hood Way signs down a steep path to reach a lake. Turn right and walk beneath the crags to return to the Visitor Centre.

POINTS OF INTEREST:
Creswell Crags – Signs of early man have been found in these caves. The Visitor Centre has a display of how they would have appeared in prehistoric times.

REFRESHMENTS:
The Olde School Tea Room, Carburton.
A limited range of refreshments is also available at the Visitor Centre.